THE

PHYNODDERREE,

AND OTHER

Legends of the Isle of Man.

BY

EDWARD CALLOW.

WITH SIXTY ILLUSTRATIONS.

Drawn expressly for this Work, and Engraved on Wood, by W. J. Watson.

London:

J. DEAN AND SON, FLEET STREET, E.C.

THE ELFINS' RIDE.—(See page 49.)

THE
PHYNODDERREE,

AND OTHER

Legends of the Isle of Man.

BY

EDWARD CALLOW.

WITH SIXTY ILLUSTRATIONS.

Drawn expressly for this Work, and Engraved on Wood, by W. J. WATSON.

FACSIMILE REPRINT 1994
LLANERCH PUBLISHERS, FELINFACH.

ISBN 1 897853 38 6

TO THE

Dear Fairies

OF MY OWN HOME,

SARAH FRANCES, FRANCES ELIZABETH,

AND

ALICE MARY,

I dedicate

THIS BOOK.

EDWARD CALLOW.

CONTENTS.

PREFACE.

N no part of the British Islands has the belief in the existence of Fairies retained a stronger hold upon the people than in the Isle of Man. In spite of the tendency of this matter-of-fact age to destroy what little of poetry, romance, and chivalry Nineteenth Century education has left to us, there lurks still in many countries, and especially in mountainous districts, a half credulity in the supernatural.

Many legends of good and evil Fairies are still related by the country people of Mona's Isle ; and those who care to inquire into the habits and customs of the Manx cottagers will see and hear much that will reward their curiosity. It is not the mere excursionist, visiting the Island for a summer holiday and keeping on the beaten track of sightseers, who will ever learn or see anything of these customs, but he who branches off the high road into the recesses of the mountain districts.

When gathering materials for the tale of the Communion Cup of Kirk Malew, I visited the Vicarage to ascertain, if possible, the date of the disappearance of the Fairy Silver Goblet, which Waldron in his "History" speaks of as being then in existence and in safe keeping in the Church. In the course of conversation on the lingering belief in Fairies, the Vicar informed me that one of his own parishioners—a regular attendant at Church, and a well-to-do farmer—had lately expressed his implicit conviction that such people as fairies *did* frequent the Glen in which he lived ; and in reply to the Parson's question, " Have you ever, in your life, seen a fairy ? " he replied, " No ! I can't exactly say I ever *saw* one ; but I've smelt them often enough."

Sir Walter Scott, in his " Peveril of the Peak," gives an outline of the legend of the " Mough-dy-Dhoo," the Phantom Black Dog of Peel Castle ; and in his notes he refers to others. Waldron, in his quaint " History of the Isle of Man," alludes to several legends, and relates a good deal that is interesting on the superstitions of the Manx people and their belief in Elves and Fairies.

To rescue from oblivion some of the legends that delighted my early years, and present them in an entertaining shape before the reader, has long been my wish ; and if, by reading them, an interest in, and a desire to visit, the beautiful Isle of Man is created in any who now only know of its existence as an island somewhere in the Irish Sea, I shall not have written in vain.

I am indebted to the late JAMES BURMAN, Esq., F.R.A.S., Secretary to the Lieut.-Governor and the Council of the Island, to the late PAUL BRIDSON, Esq., Honorary Secretary to the Manx Society, and others, for many of the materials of these tales.

In the event of these tales being favourably received I shall be encouraged to repeat this experiment, as there are many more Legends of the Isle of Man that I am inclined to hope will be found both interesting and entertaining.

HIGHGATE, *July*, 1882.   EDWARD CALLOW.

THE LIST
of the
ILLUSTRATIONS

Ah, Mona's isle, fair Mona's isle,
No land so dear as thou to me :
Thy gorse and heather covered hills,
With waterfalls and sparkling rills,
Which join the bright green sea.

I love to wander in solitude
By the banks of thy gurgling streams,
Or sit and muse on a mossy stone
Of fairy-lore, buggane, and gnome,
Screen'd from the sungod's beams.

'Tis sweet to ramble alone,
At eve o'er the silvery sand,
Watching the waves in the moonlight gleam,
Now here, now there, in frolic they seem
To coyley kiss the land.

Each valley, mountain, and glen,
Waterfall, streamlet, and sea,
Cavern, rock, harbour, and bay,
Last home of the Elfin and Fay,
Fair Mona, are all dear to me.

" Then take the air,
With a butterfly pair
Linked to a petal blue."—See page 53.

THE PHYNODDERREE:

A TALE OF FAIRY LOVE.

CHAPTER I.

*" I must not think, I may not gaze
On what I am, on what I was."*

BYRON.

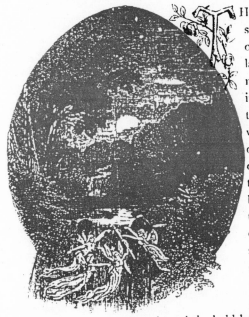

THE wide open Bay of Ramsey, on the northern coast of the Isle of Man, is the largest and safest of all the many anchorages surrounding the shores of this beautiful island. It affords a welcome shelter to vessels of all sizes, from the little coasting hooker of thirty tons to the leviathan Atlantic steamship of three thousand : and it is no uncommon sight, during the season of westerly gales, to see upwards of two hundred ships, large and small, snugly and safely riding at anchor under the lee of North Barrule and the bold headland of St. Maughold.

North Barrule rises some eighteen hundred feet high, and pierces, with his conical sugarloaf-shaped head, the hurrying clouds as they are driven before the gale. It terminates the mountain range that forms the back-bone of the Isle of Mona, or, as it is called in the native tongue, *Ellan Vannin*.

Although North Barrule always forms a grand and distinctive feature in the landscape of the northern part of the island, it is not when viewed from the shore that it is seen to its greatest advantage, but from the sea ; and many a traveller, when approaching the island from the Cumberland coast, must have been struck with its resemblance in shape to Vesuvius.

Many are the streams that take their rise from the rocks and slopes of North Barrule, and, winding down and leaping from craig to craig, after uniting with each other in one or other of the lower glens, find their way at last into the sea. The largest of these is the Sulby River, which, after leaving the romantic glen of that name, becomes a considerable stream, winding for some distance at the base of the mountain dividing it from the low sandy plain that stretches away northwards, till it terminates in the Point of Ayre—the nearest approach of the island to the Scottish coast—falls into the sea, forming ere it reaches there a convenient har-bour, upon which is built the northern capital of the island, Ramsey, which gives its name to the capacious bay.

Besides Sulby there are two other notable glens, up whose rugged ways the visitor desirous of climbing the mountain has to wend his way. One of these, Ballure, is of surpassing beauty, with its dancing, dashing stream fighting its way, jealous of its greater rival of Sulby, round about and over rocks, between the crevices of which the most exquisite ferns grow in the greatest profusion and array, to find an independent outlet to the sea. The other is the Glen of Aldyn, whither I would take my reader, while I relate to him the sad story of the Phynodderree.

Very many years ago, long prior to the days of parish registers, and before Manx people kept written chronicles or diaries of their daily lives, there resided in a little thatch-covered cottage about half-way up Glen

Aldyn, an old man, who cultivated a small patch of ground, fed a few mountain sheep, and kept a solitary cow. In his farming avocations—in which, when not engaged with her spinning-wheel, his only daughter, Kitty, assisted him—old Billy Nell, or William Kerruish, added that of tailor; and as the best tailor for miles round Kerruish was famed. He himself imagined, in the simplicity of his heart, it was to the good quality of his work, his moderate charges, and the excellence of his materials he owed this reputation, and so much business that he had hard work to find time for that and his farming duties too. Mrs. Joughin, the wife of a tailor in Ramsey, told her neighbours "that old Kerruish was only a botcher, and knew no more about tailoring than his own cow; and that if his bold-faced girl, Kitty, didn't encourage the young fellows with her smirks and her smiles, ne'er one of 'em would ever give him a job."

Mrs. Joughin was not altogether calculated to give an unbiassed opinion on the subject, and her observations were looked upon as somewhat prejudiced. At any rate, though old Billy Nell's style might not have been quite equal to that of the Pooles and Smallpages of Douglas and Castletown, the young men of Maughold and Lezayre were only too glad to give him their custom, if only to have an excuse to visit his cottage, and, if possible, pass a few words with, and obtain a favouring smile from, his fair daughter Kitty.

The old tailor-farmer was known among his neighbours by the name of Billy Nell, to distinguish him from several other William Kerruishes in the parish, his mother's name having been Ellen; his *soubriquet* meaning William, the son of Ellen.

The innuendo against Kitty conveyed by Mrs. Joughin's uncharitable remarks as to smirks and smiles was unjust in every way. Kitty was as good as she was beautiful. Such laughing, deep blue eyes, with long silken lashes that would have made an Eastern beauty die of envy; rich, dark-brown luxuriant tresses, well-developed pencilled eyebrows; and cheeks that rose and lily combined to render perfect, with full luscious lips and teeth that dazzled with their whiteness, together with a lithe and graceful

KITTY KERRUISH AND HER FAIRY LOVER.

"*Sometimes I saw you sit and spin;
And in the pauses of the wind,
Sometimes I heard you sing.*"

                                        TENNYSON.

figure, afforded a good excuse for any young man taking the longest walk to gaze upon ; and when to all these were added the sweetest expression and that indefinable charm that ever attaches itself to a really good and pure-minded woman, little was the wonder she had enslaved the hearts of all the young fishermen and farmers between Kirk Maughold and the Point of Ayre. However hard the wind may have blown at night, and the young fishermen may have had to toil, before bringing their frail barques and catches of herrings safe into harbour, it was no fatigue to them to walk out to Glen Aldyn to catch a sight of fair Kitty's face, and maybe have a few words of pleasant talk, or hear her sing, for Kitty sang sweetly, so sweetly that in the summer twilight, as she sang to her father at his work, while she plied her spinning-wheel, the fairies would come and hide themselves behind the trees or amid the tall waving corn to listen to her voice with rapt attention.

Sometimes when she was singing thus, surrounded by her wee and invisible listeners, a sound would strike their sensitive ears, the sound of the approaching footsteps of some one coming up the glen. They would all scatter right and left, and, though unseen by Kitty or her father, would cause such a fluttering among the graceful ferns and amid the drooping flowers of the fuchsia trees that shrouded the cottage from the roadway, as would make Kitty think it was some sudden breeze of wind from the mountain-top, the sure precursor of a change of weather. The approaching step would probably be that of Evan Christian, or Robert Faragher, the two most persevering of all her wooers ; the former of whom was never too tired to trudge from Lewaigue, or the latter all the way from Ballasaig, to pay her a visit and plead his cause.

To both of them, as well as to all the young gallants who flocked to her father's cottage on some pretence or other, Kitty Kerruish turned a deaf ear. A kind word and a sweet smile she always had for every one, and would listen to their compliments and praises with a modesty that only still further inflamed their hearts ; but when they ventured to speak to her of love, she would shake her head, laugh, and adroitly turn the conversation. When Evan Christian ventured once to press his suit with more than customary boldness, making profession of his love and begging for. hers in return, she firmly but kindly replied : " No, Evan ; whilst my dear father lives, I can never leave him. At present he has all the love I have to give away."

ONE summer evening Kitty was seated as usual under the shade of the fuchsia trees at the cottage door, her delicate fingers busy with the yarn, while her spinning-wheel whirled round and round with a pleasant and homely hum, its treadle worked with the prettiest little foot in the island. Old Kerruish had gone to the DOONEY-MOOAR, the great man of the parish of Ballaugh, to carry home some work he had just completed, and Kitty was singing to herself a sweet, plaintive air, while awaiting his return.

Pausing in her song, she turned her head, the better to listen for the old man's footsteps as he came up the glen, when she suddenly saw, standing beside her, what she took to be a little child. Her first impression was that it was one of neighbour Mylrea's children, who had wandered up the glen from the valley below, having come up the course of the stream, as the little ones frequently did, in search of trout, which they had a dexterous and somewhat unorthodox method of catching, by means of routing about under the stones with a stick, and frightening the fish into a rudely-constructed hand-net.

A second glance at once showed her she was mistaken. It was not little Tommy Mylrea. What stood before her was no mortal child, but a little fairy mannikin of most gallant and graceful bearing. Kitty had never before seen anything so charming or imagined aught so lovely.

"Sweet maid," said he, taking her hand in his and raising it to his lips with a grace and style that would have been envied by any gentleman of the court of the "Grand Monarque," "continue thy song, and be not in the least alarmed."

"Who and what are you?" she exclaimed, withdrawing her hand from his impassioned grasp, and feeling, in spite of an inner conviction, that he was hardly a "canny" visitor, most agreeably impressed by the wee creature's face and manner.

"Lovely Kitty—*Ben-my-chree*—I am your most devoted admirer, your slave. In me you see no mortal, but a fairy mannikin, whose heart has for long past been truant to his race, and devoted, oh, I cannot tell how truly and intensely fixed on

UDDEREEK.

thee. Nay, sweet maiden," continued the little man, again seizing her hand, and overcoming the coy resistance she at first displayed, "I would not harm thee for all the elfin world. Often and often have I watched thee here, and witnessed how thou hast heard, unheeded, the rhapsodies poured into thine ear by the mortal admirers of thy wondrous and unequalled beauty, as they have offered thee their love. I was here when Evan Christian urged his suit, and was sent away with a bitter and bad feeling in his heart, and the knowledge that only on your father's death. can he have any hopes of gaining your affection. I looked on from under yonder hart's-tongue fern when Bob Faragher vowed he would work his fingers to the bone for you, and prayed you to become the mistress of Ballasaig. I saw his dejected look and heard his heavy sigh, as before turning down the glen by the peat-stack, he cast a parting and a longing look as you carried your spinning-wheel into the cottage. I have heard all their avowals, and seen how each one has been refused. Oh, how I chuckled as I saw them depart, baffled and disappointed; but my heart, sweet Kitty, my love, is beyond them all. Nothing that any mortal, any mere man, ever felt or can feel at all approaches the intense adoration, the worship I now offer to you, dear Kitty—*Mooar-Ben-my-chree*—and that love I now lay at your feet."

The poor girl was utterly powerless to resist so passionate and so earnest an appeal as the handsome little mannikin poured forth with a volubility that admitted of no interruption. His presence completely fascinated and overpowered her. It seemèd as if her heart, which had so long and so stoutly withstood the assaults of all her mortal swains, was suddenly captured by the *coup de main* of her elfin lover. She was spell-bound, and had at once to give way before his impetuous attack, and surrender at discretion. Her whole inner being was changed. She felt that now, but never before, she knew what love—fiery, intense, passionate, consuming love—really was. It took possession of her whole soul. The dart of Cupid had pierced her lovely bosom to the very haft. The tender but all-potent passion had absorbed her life and taken entire possession of her very existence. She felt a perfect agony of pleasure, as with wrapt attention to his every word and all oblivious to everything around but him, she listened while he continued to address her.

" Hear me, dearest maid, and let me plead my cause. I hold a high position at my elfin sovereign's court, and the fairest of our fairy maids in vain display their beauteous charms to me. Thou, sweet Kitty, and thou alone, possess the love, the heart of Uddereek."

Springing lightly up on to her spinning-wheel, the little lover threw his arms around her neck and passionately covered her sweet, rosy, pouting lips with his fervent kisses.

Kitty was enthralled, and unresistingly submitted to the gallant Uddereek's love, ardent as it was, and it was with feelings akin to deep regret that after a while, when the sound of her father's footsteps were heard coming up the glen, she saw him making preparations to depart. " Hark ! What sounds are those? I must now away. Kitty, *Ben-my-chree,* I hear thy father drawing near. No one must be. a witness to our love. Should it e'er be known at the elfin court that I have dared to love, or even, *Fact-y-tooil-graigh,* cast a longing eye on mortal maid, I know not what dreadful fate might befall me. But, *Kitty-ma-cushla* (my darling Kitty), for thee and thy love I would risk all, if it were a thousandfold as much, and brave the direst vengeance of the fairy power. But the better to keep the secret, both from mortal and fairy ken, of our meetings and our love, I will await thee, my own, each evening at the twilight hour under the blue rowan tree in the *Magher-Glass,* Glen Aldyn (in the green field of Glen Aldyn), down there in the valley, beside where the limpid stream springs frisking o'er the rocks and dashes down into the lower *Gully-Mooar.*"

Once again clasping her in his tiny arms and impressing a passionate kiss upon her lips, and murmuring a soft, tender farewell, he vanished from before her as suddenly as he came.

Kitty, who thought she had fallen asleep, and that all had been a glorious and delicious dream, sat entranced and musing after he had gone, gazing intently on the spot where Uddereek had disappeared. She felt half pleased half frightened at the new, strange sensation her heart now for the first time experienced. On the morning of that day she had risen a simple girl ; now she was a perfect woman, with all a woman's feelings. She felt, come weal, come woe, her whole future existence was bound up in that of her elfin lover. She sat on gazing vacantly before her, and when old Billy Nell drew near the cottage and gave the accustomed signal of his return home, he was surprised at its not being answered, and at hearing nought of Kitty's voice. He turned into the garden, but instead of her hurrying forward to meet him as was her wont, she was sitting silent and still, looking vacantly into space. No blithesome song, no busy truddle of the spinning-wheel as usual welcomed the old man's return. The distaff was on the ground at her feet, the wheel was overturned and lay against the house wall, where the fairy man had cast it when he sprang away in his flight; the yarn was broken and entangled, and Kitty sat utterly heedless of his approach.

She noticed him not, but her lips moved. He approached her and listened, as she gently murmured—

" *Ogh-cha-nee*, Woe's me. *Ta-graigh-ayn*, I love him."

The old man listened with astonishment to her mutterings. He called her by name, and instantly she jumped up, and, passing her hands before her eyes, as if awakening out of a trance or sleep, she welcomed him home in her old fond loving way, and after relieving him of his staff and kelpie, hastened to prepare their frugal evening meal of griddle cakes made of placket meal and salt herrings, washed down with fresh butter-milk and followed by a dish of *Pinjean* (*Anglice*, curds-and-whey), for the making of which in perfection Kitty was famous.

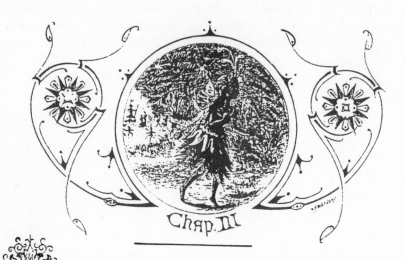

Chap. II

VERY evening, punctually as the twilight hour approached, did Kitty Kerruish feel an irresistible fascination steal over her that drew her to the trysting-place under the blue rowan tree in the *Magher-Glass* of Glen Aldyn to meet her elfin lover; and there she would sit, listening with rapture to the passionate and extatic avowals of his love, mingled with the most eloquent praises of her beauty, which the mannikin gently whispered into her intoxicated ear, as he lay like some fair child upon her lap, with his arms encircled round her neck.

One evening, to tease her lover—for Kitty, like all her sex, dearly loved to tease—she told him she did not half believe his protestations of affection, and that he would not be willing to make any great sacrifice to prove them.

Uddereek vowed she wronged him, and called upon her to name any test, any sacrifice she wanted him to make. At that moment she either could not or would not think of any; but presently he mentioned that the following night the fairy king and queen would hold a grand court and feast in Glen Rushen, in the southern part of the island, near Ballasalla, in honour of RE-HOLLYS-VOOAR-YN-ONYR, the royal festival of the harvest moon, and that every elfin in Ellan Vannin would have to attend. He

MAGHER-GLASS OF GLEN RUSHEN.

described to her wondering and delighted ear how the dancing would be kept up till the moon ceased to shine, and sank behind the head of South Barrule, and the ruddy rays of the coming sun began to show signs of rising from the eastern sea.

"Ah, Uddereek!" said Kitty, teasingly, "you will enjoy all that, and soon forget, for the time at any rate, all about me, or that you ever saw or thought of poor Kitty."

"No, *Cushla*," the little man replied. "I shall be alone amid the elfin throng, and in spite of all the feasting and the music, all the dancing in the ring, all the revels in the ferns and sweet wild flowers, I shall wish myself far away from it all, and long to be with thee, dear Kitty."

"I just don't believe one word about it," she said, laughingly, and still intent on plaguing her little elfin lover. "Some fairy maid, whose beauty far surpasses mine, will captivate your heart, and you will soon forget your mortal love."

"Never! never!" he hastily interrupted. "I swear, my darling, never! And to prove to you how false and how unjust are your suspicions, I will leave the elfin gambols, and immediately the king and queen have risen from the feast and the revels have fairly commenced, will slip away, and meet you here, dearest Kitty, three hours after the sun has set."

No woman but would have been pleased and satisfied at such a proof of her power and attractions, and Kitty Kerruish felt gratified and delighted as she laughingly replied—

"I will be here to meet you; and mind, sir, I shall expect you."

Little did she dream, poor lass! of the dire consequences that would result from his temerity and her exactitude, or at how dear a cost to both of them this proof of his love would be obtained.

REAT were the preparations the next evening among the Elfin community for the coming feast and dance in the *Magher-Glass* of Glen Rushen.

Fairies from all parts of the island assembled to do honour to their Elfin monarch and his beauteous queen. Even the arch and naughty bugganes had to be upon their good behaviour, and for the time leave off their mischief and their pranks.

The feast, which was of the most *récherché* description, did credit to the fairy Gunters, whose successful endeavours elicited the praise of every elfin *bon vivant*. Unfortunately, the *menu* was transcribed with humming-bird quill upon a rose-leaf, which withered and curled up before the next day's sun had reached its meridian, so that no permanent record was left of the various *plats* and *entrées* placed before the guests ; but we may be sure that on so auspicious an occasion, like a Mansion House or Guildhall banquet, "every delicacy in season" was provided, together with wines of the "rarest vintages."

The sparkling wine-cup passed busily and merrily round the board, well attended by jest and song. Many were the tales told that night of tricks and exploits, played by mischief-loving sprites and bugganes on such sinning mortals as had offended them, either by coming unbidden across their path, or neglecting one of the many customs and offerings which old usage had sanctified, and the wee folk considered to be their due, and in consequence had drawn down the fairy wrath upon their unlucky heads.

When the elfin party had done full justice to all the good things before them, and before adjourning for the festive dance, the royal healths were proposed and drank with all the honours, and the old Glen of Rushen rang again as the little voices shouted forth their homage to the toast. Seated next to Uddereek was a beauteous being who would, if seen by mortal man, have captivated him at once and completely turned his brain. Could any modern photographer but have obtained a negative of her fairy form and figure, the market for professional beauties' *cartes de visites* would have simply declined to far below zero, and the happy man would have realized a fortune.

This fairy beauty flirted—oh, flirting is but too mild a term to apply to her attacks upon our little Uddereek. In spite, however, of her blandishments most lavishly bestowed, and the many little wilful, winning ways, so well—ah! too well—known to all the sex who are on conquest bent, whether they be fairies or no, denizens in Ellan Vannin or Belgravia—Uddereek was true to his mortal love of Glen Aldyn, and remained proof against them all, confining himself only to such attentions as no gentleman, elfin or mortal, could refuse to a lady seated beside him, and especially so fair as she.

Had the lovely Estella been born in Mayfair she could not have displayed more perfect *ton*, and no young lady in her second season, placed by a judicious and worldly-wise mamma beside the most eligible *parti* in the room, could have been more scientific in her attacks upon him. Her most bewitching smiles, her most love-inspiring glances, darted adroitly over the rim of her fan, composed of a single leaf from a magnificent dark purple pansy, and all the arts of the most accomplished coquetry were launched forth with a ravishing abandon, but all in vain. The heart of the elfin Uddereek was true as steel.

The powerful battery of her expressive eyes seemed utterly to fail in

UDDEREEK AND ESTELLA.

obtaining the proper range and elevation. Every shot, every dart, well directed as it was, fell short of its mark, and Uddereek was unscathed. He was cool, composed, gentlemanly, and aggravatingly polite.

Knowing full well her own powers, she felt stung to the quick at such a failure as she had never experienced before. She was simply astonished, almost stupefied, at such a result. At first she thought she must be seated beside a fool, one of those unimpressionable dolts too frequently met with in all societies, even of the best, who have no soul, no appreciation for anything. A second glance convinced her of the folly of such a thought.

3

Besides, was not the elfin next to her, Uddereek, the wittiest, the most accomplished, and most gallant little gentleman in the elfin court?

Estella looked jealously around to see if there was any other fairy maid at whom she could detect him gazing. She sought in vain for any one there, she would condescend to admit for one moment to herself, could possibly be regarded as a rival. She knew full well her own transcendent beauty, and that all acknowledged her the belle of the *fête*. Still she was far—very far—from being satisfied, and felt confident that no heart not already bestowed upon another could resist such charms and withstand such advances as hers. Her pride was piqued, her vanity deeply wounded, her curiosity excited, and she determined to fathom the mystery.

The feast over, the ball began. They one and all stood up. The king and queen led off the lively reel. Uddereek handed the fair Estella through the mazes of the dance, during which, far from desisting, she renewed with, if possible, redoubled energy her attacks, tried afresh all her arts to bring him to her feet, took skilful advantage of every little incident of the dance to bewitch him, but all in vain.

The dance ended—even a country dance, a true Roger de Coverley, must, some time or other, come to a finish—he led her to a seat upon a moss-grown bank, shadowed over with ferns of the daintiest kind, and making some excuse, slipped hurriedly away from the glen, to meet his Kitty at the blue rowan tree, where he knew so well she would be waiting his arrival. Uddereek, hoping he had left the elfin throng unnoticed and unmissed, hied him quick as the lightning flash, upon the swift wings of hot young love, from Rushen Glen to Aldyn.

Estella felt mortified by her failure, and insulted by the nonchalant behaviour and indifference of Uddereek to her charms and beauty, which even her attentions to him had not prevented her from seeing had been admiringly gazed upon by many another elfin swain who had envied Uddereek his great good fortune in sitting next to her, and would have given anything, even the tips of their tiny moustaches, to have had half the sweet blandishments bestowed upon them that had been thrown away upon his unsympathizing heart. She was deeply hurt and thirsted for revenge. That there was a mystery somewhere she was certain, and that a rival who had already full possession of his heart existed, she was fully convinced, or he never could have so withstood such sweet sorcery as she had tried upon him. To discover that rival was now the work before her. She watched his every movement, and his departure, stealthy though it was, did not escape her eye. Prompted by her natural womanly curiosity, and instigated by all the jealous feelings of a revengeful heart, she swiftly followed on his trail.

ITTY KERRUISH was true to her appointment at the blue rowan tree, and had been waiting some few minutes when Uddereek arrived. After returning his fond embrace, she began to upbraid her elfin lover for his late arrival, jestingly twitting him with his inability to tear himself away from the fair demoiselles of the fairy court; when, as he was stopping her upbraidings by tender kisses, expostulating with her for one instant doubting the sincerity of his love, a rustling was heard among the long grass and the ferns, and before escape could be even thought of they were surrounded instantly by a swarm of fairy guards.

The rejected and jealous Estella had but too surely followed him to the trysting-place, and there she saw enough to show her who and what her hated rival was. With all her despised and rejected love turned into the bitterest hate, and urged on by her deeply wounded pride, she determined on prompt action and most terrible revenge. Swift as the meteor's flight did she return to the elfin revels, bounding o'er mountains, from peak to peak of North Barrule, Snaefell, Pennyphot, and Grebah, away to South Barrule, and thence down the valley to Glen Rushen, where she laid before the king and his astonished court the news that Uddereek—the noble and modest Uddereek forsooth—the pattern-good-young-man of the elfin race, had dared to love a mortal, and now, even now, at that very moment, instead of attending on his royal master at the RE-HOLLYS-VOOAR-YN-ONYR, as was his bounden duty, he was seated in her lap beneath the blue rowan tree in the *Magher-Glass* of Glen Aldyn, pouring fourth his forbidden vows of love.

Such news caused the greatest consternation and surprise. The announcement to a conclave of tonsured monks, that one of their number had been " asked in church," could not have been received with more astonishment. Uddereek was so well known, so beloved by all, and stood so high in his sovereign's favour, that the intelligence of his defection came like a thunderbolt among them.

All dancing ceased. The very minstrels suddenly hushed their strains, and the ball abruptly ended. The king and the whole court were struck dumb with horror and amazement at such an unheard-of breach of fairy etiquette, such a flagrant departure from the rules of all elfin decorum.

The outraged monarch gave command for the immediate pursuit, and, putting himself at the head of his fairy guards, started off on the pinions of the evening breeze to seize the culprit who had dared to so transgress the elfin laws.

Estella, whose jealousy was now about to have its sweet reward, and all whose " rejected addresses " were to be so amply revenged, was but too good a guide in pointing out the exact spot where to find the guilty pair.

Uddereek was instantly torn from the embrace of the frightened Kitty, and ruthlessly hurried off to trial.

The king and all his court, at least all the male portion of the retinue, could not help paying a gallant and flattering tribute to the surpassing beauty of the mortal maid who had enslaved their truant comrade, and openly expressed their admiration of the sweet Kitty Kerruish. Their

UDDEREEK SEIZED BY THE FAIRY GUARDS.

openly expressed encomiums of the fair maiden were not altogether approved or endorsed by the little lady fairies; and the queen herself was seen to change colour and fan herself with more than usual vigour as she noticed how her royal spouse stood gazing all too admiringly upon poor Uddereek's lovely enslaver.

As for Estella, all this undisguised admiration of her hated rival only increased her rage beyond all bounds, and she passionately entreated the fairy monarch to visit the poor girl with the most instant and horrible vengeance in the elfin power to inflict. That, however, he resolutely and gallantly refused to do; but turning from the furious fairy to the trembling mortal, he thus addressed her: "Most fair but erring mortal, my heart is too chivalrous to punish you as requested by this furious and jealous fairy. Indeed, I can quite excuse, and almost pardon, the rash Uddereek the error he has been guilty of; for never did I behold a mortal maiden so beautiful before. I wish it was within the limits of my mystic power to transform thee into a fairy maid, for I would do so."

On hearing this the queen looked anything than either pleased or flattered, and her verbena-leaf fan went faster than ever, while she and also most of the ladies and beauties of the court felt very well pleased and contented that their monarch's powers were so limited, and that they were safe from the advent amongst their ranks of so dangerous a rival.

"You must, however," continued the king to Kitty, and unheeding the disapproval of his remarks expressed so plainly by his royal consort's looks and undisguised annoyance—"you must depart from Ellan Vannin and leave the island for ever, never to return, for if you are found upon its shores at the rising of the next new moon you will be at this lady's mercy," pointing to the fuming Estella, "and I cannot aid or protect you from her vengeful power. So farewell, and take heed; fly from her machinations and depart from hence."

In a moment Kitty was alone. King, court, fairy guards, and Uddereek had all vanished. The last to disappear was the rejected but now triumphant Estella, who lingered to cast upon her fair mortal rival a look in which was concentrated the most exulting revenge and the intensest hatred.

* * * * * *

Kitty Kerruish could not forget her elfin love, though she tried to think it all a dream. She came night after night, heedless of the elfin king's warning, to sit under the blue rowan tree in the *Magher-Glass* of Glen Aldyn, there to sit in hopes of Uddereek's return.

The rising of the next new moon found her still true to her love at the old trysting-place, but, alas! for the last time. Her spiteful elfin rival was there too; and now having poor Kitty in her power she proceeded to execute her vengeance in a most sure and subtle way. She caused a noxious mist to rise from the damp ground of the Glen—a mist loaded with the vapours of nightshade, henbane, and every deadly and poisonous plant she could collect. The mist, unnoticed by poor Kitty, spread round her, and every sigh for her lost fairy lover was but the means of taking a fresh draught of the insidious poison, till, feeling chilled by what she innocently thought the evening air, she reluctantly left the Glen and slowly turned her footsteps home.

The fated vapour had too surely done its work. Estella was avenged. From that night the health of the tailor's daughter was gone—her very life was sapped. Slowly she pined away till the evening of the next new moon, when poor old Billy Nell sat beside the couch of his darling child as her sweet spirit calmly took its flight.

* * * * * *

For Uddereek a different and even worse fate was in store. He was formally tried by his peers and condemned to banishment from the fairy community, to remain a lonely wanderer in Ellan Vannin till the crack of doom. His sentence was no sooner pronounced by the king than Uddereek was instantly changed from his beautiful elfin form into a figure resembling a satyr, half boy half billy-goat, from whence he derives his present name of PHYNODDERREE, or HAIRY ONE.

He has remained in the Isle of Man ever since—at least until a very recent date ; but after the introduction of railways into the island neither Phynodderree nor fairy of any kind has ever been met with by any sober man. It is currently supposed by the Manx people that the shrill, discordant blast of the railway whistle has been more than the delicate aural organs of so sensitive a race as the fairies could stand, and that, disgusted with the inventions of men and the introduction of board schools and other so-called improvements, they have taken their departure from the shores of Mona's Isle for ever, flying to some land where civilization is not so far advanced, and where life is not conducted upon such high-pressure principles as it now is in the British Isles.

The Phynodderree, before his flight from the island, delighted in good-naturedly assisting those whom he befriended, and many are the tales told of the little fellow's beneficence.

To help an industrious farmer or fisherman was Phynodderree's greatest pleasure. For one he would reap his crops in a single night ; or if he wanted to build a wall or a cow-shed, would convey stone enough between sunset and sunrise to the required spot to enable him to complete his work. For a favoured fisherman he would repair his nets or boat whilst the owner slept.

One man, desirous of showing his gratitude to the good-natured little creature for his work of conveying stones from a quarry, with which to build a house, and remembering he was naked, thought some clothes would be acceptable, and so took a suit and laid them on a place where he was supposed to frequent. Phynodderree on finding them took them up one by one, and throwing each garment away over his shoulder as he named it, gave vent to his feelings in his native Manx, exclaimed—

> " *Bayrn da'n choine, dy doogh da'n choine!*
> *Cooat d'an dreeyn, dy, doogh d'an dreeyn!*
> *Breechyn d'an toyn, dy, doogh da'n toyn!*
> *Agh my she Chiat ooily, shoh cha nee Chiat Glen reagh Rushen.*"

The literal English translation of which is—

> "Cap for the head, alas, poor head !
> Coat for the back, alas, poor back !
> Breeches for the breech, alas, poor breech !
> If all these be thine, thine then cannot be the merry Glen of Rushen ; "

and away he went with a melancholy cry that was heard far away over the glens and valleys, leaving all the fine clothes behind him.

Any man who through industry and attention to his business made good progress in the world and thrived, was said by the Manx country folk to have been favoured and helped by Phynodderree.

When badly treated or provoked, Phynodderree could be spiteful, and an instance is recorded of his having shown this side of his character to a farmer whose field he had mown for him. The ungrateful man grumbled and found fault with the way it was done, saying he could have done it better himself. This enraged Phynodderree, who waited till next year, and when the farmer set to work to mow it he came with a scythe in his hand and chased him off the field. For many years after this the grass remained uncut, every one being afraid to attempt to mow it.

During the Civil War, when the island was occupied by the Parliamentary army, a trooper, having heard the reason of the grass being left uncut, volunteered to mow it himself. He proceeded to the middle of the field and commenced mowing all round him in a circle. Phynodderree set to work as well, and with such vigour that the soldier had great difficulty to prevent him cutting his legs off. He persevered, however, keeping a sharp look out on his elfin fellow workman, till at last it was completed.

The Manx Phynodderree was evidently much the same kind of being as the Lubber Fiend mentioned by Milton in his " L'Allegro," and also the Scottish Brownie and the Swart-Alfar of Edda in the German.

In conclusion, I will quote the words of a well-known poet in describing him and his charitable work :

> " Ah, Phynodderree !
> His was the wizard hand that toiled
> At midnight witching hour,
> That gathered the sheep from the coming storm,

Ere the shepherd saw it lour ;
Yet asked no fee, save a scattered sheaf
From the peasant's garnered hoard,
Or a cream bowl, pressed by virgin lip,
To be left on the household board."

Again, in allusion to the sad fate of his mortal love, and the long, long lament of his true heart for poor Kitty Kerruish, the same delightful writer says :

"You may hear his voice on the desert hill, ·
Where the mountain winds have power ;
'Tis a wild lament for his buried love,
And his long-lost fairy bower."

Tom Kewley and the Lannanshee;

OR,

THE FAIRY CUP OF KIRK MALEW.

CHAPTER I.

BALLASALLA is a quiet little Manx village on the bank of a rushing, leaping, murmuring trout stream, which, after tearing down from the sides of South Barrule mountain, and winding in and out between the stone boulders, and through the nooks and glens abounding in this part of the island, eventually finds its way into the sea at Castletown, some two miles distant, there mingling its pure fresh waters with those of the "briny deep" close beneath the old grey limestone walls of Castle Rushen. On the opposite side of the stream to the village are the venerable ruins of what was, many years ago, the proud and stately Rushen Abbey, the wealthiest monastic establishment in the Isle of Man ;

and between whose cloistered vaults and the dark dungeons of Castle Rushen, tradition says there once existed a secret subterranean passage, whose walls, had they tongues as well as the ears attributed to mural constructions, could doubtless tell many a dismal tale of persecution and wrong.

In a cottage in the outskirts of Ballasalla, and removed but a few paces from the Douglas road, dwelt, many years ago, one Tom Kewley with his wife and one child. Tom was an honest fellow, and as industrious as most of his neighbours, cultivating a patch of land, hardly of extent sufficient to be called a farm, and occasionally, especially in the herring season, taking a turn as one of the crew of a Peel or Port-le-Mary fishing lugger.

Kewley might have been a more thriving man than he was but for the failing he shared with so many of his neighbours—a liking for jovial company, and not knowing when he had had enough of strong drink. The consequence was that many a groat and many an hour were wasted with boon companions that might have been employed otherwise, to the great advantage of himself and family.

One evening in the early autumn Tom was trudging towards his home after visiting his fields, whither he had been to see how soon his crops would be ready for the sickle, when, casting his eye over his shoulder to watch some clouds gathering upon the mountain top, which, he feared, portended a storm not very favourable to his little expected harvest, his attention was arrested by seeing a cloud of white mist apparently roll from under a dark, threatening cloud hanging on the mountain side. This mist had an appearance different to anything he had ever noticed before, and while gazing at it he thought he perceived the figure of a man emerge from it, waving his arms in a frantic manner, and running with all speed down the hillside towards the village. He stood and watched attentively what, at first, he thought must be some supernatural being; but as the man drew nearer, hurrying on and scrambling over every obstacle in his way, Tom thought he recognized the figure, and, mounting to the top of a stone wall to get a better view, he himself became visible to the running man, who altered his course and hastened on towards him with increased speed, shouting at the top of his voice. As the fugitive—for there could be no doubt he was one, and flying for his life—approached nearer, Kewley recognized him as Philip Caine, a pedlar, who travelled the island over, from end to end and from one side to the other, with his pack of useful and tempting articles ; and who was always a welcome guest, go where he would, for he ever had a budget full of news as well as wares.

" Phil ! is that yourself? and what's your haste, man? You couldn't run faster or look more scared if a buggane, or Cuttar McCulloch himself, were at your heels. What on earth's the matter ? Speak, man."

The flying pedlar could give no reply. He was far too exhausted with his run down the mountain side to speak, and stood clinging to Tom's arm panting for breath, and looking as Tom had said, " scared," and as if he feared being followed and snatched away by some uncanny arm.

"Where's your pack, Phil?" asked Kewley, seeing he was without his usual burden. " Is it robbed you've been, is it ? "

" Robbed and murdered," gasped the pedlar, and sank into a sitting posture on the ground.

" Nonsense, man," rejoined Tom, with a laugh. " Murdered men don't run like you did. Come in the house and rest awhile. Maybe ye'll be able to tell us all what's befell ye."

Peggy Kewley was not a little surprised on seeing the scared pedlar enter the cottage door with her husband, and it was not until Phil Caine had rested some time and partaken of supper that he could give any collected account of what had befallen him.

He had set out in the early morning from Peel with the intention of working his way to Castletown, calling at the different villages and farms on his way to dispose of his wares. His route lay over South Barrule, and after visiting St. John's, where he had done some good trade, he strapped his pack upon his shoulders, and started to cross the mountain. On and on, ever upward, Philip Caine wended his way,

4

bending beneath the burden of his pack as he trod the steep ascent. Presently, after leaving the last house on the northern side of the mountain, and nearing the highest part of the tract, that here served the purposes of roadway, he became suddenly enveloped in a dense cloud ; but this was no unusual occurrence on such high ground, and Caine thought nothing of it, and knowing by the peculiar fineness of the grass that he must be very near the summit, he continued his journey without fear.

The clouds getting denser, he stopped for a while to rest and take breath for further progress, and then discovered he had wandered from the roadway. The short soft grass being pleasanter to walk upon than the stony road, he had chosen it, and had not noticed the fact of his having strayed from the road till he discovered he had actually lost his way. He waited patiently for some time resting, and thinking that ere long the clouds would disperse ; but, to his surprise and dismay, they grew denser and denser, till at last, although he knew it still wanted several hours of sundown, it became as dark as night, and he could not distinguish any object twenty yards away.

While conjecturing what he could do, and fearing every instant the bursting of a violent storm, he watched eagerly all round for any indications of a break in the darkness, some ray of light. Presently the cloud gradually began to break and pass away. Slowly did the darkness dissipate and the light return, revealing as it did so to his astonished gaze a mighty castle, with tower above tower, battlemented walls, and all the splendour of a royal residence, in comparison with which Castle Rushen was a mere hovel. Never had he beheld so vast, so magnificent a building, but what it was, and how it came there, he could not at all imagine. He knew full well no such castle had ever been there before, and he had travelled the same road scores of times. On looking to see if he could discover any entrance or signs of life, he saw a large open courtyard, flanked on either side with extensive corridors and piazzas. At the further side was an open door, but no signs of life except a few tame pigeons that took no notice of him as they flew about, and occasionally alighted on the ground in search of food. The door was wide open, but he dare not enter it. All was quiet and death-like. Not a sound was heard. The very pigeons flew noiselessly, the flutter of their wings being like everything around them, silent. He plucked up courage as the desire to sell his wares predominated over his first fears, and determined to wait outside in the courtyard to take advantage of any one's appearing whom he could induce to become a customer. He feared to enter, lest he should be turned out neck and crop, or perhaps seized and charged with doing so for some unlawful purpose. After waiting some time, and no one appearing, he sat himself down in full view of the door, so as to see any one who might come out. Feeling hungry as well as tired, he opened a small wallet, and taking out some bread, meat, and a little pinch of salt screwed up in paper, he proceeded to make himself comfortable and enjoy his meal. Scarcely had he commenced when he heard the strains of soft music within the castle; and after listening for some moments, the sounds of clattering footsteps were heard approaching down the hall towards the door. Before he could clear up the remnants of his repast and repack his wallet, which he proceeded in all haste to do, a weird and ghastly figure appeared, revealing as it emerged from the door and turned its head towards the horrified Philip Caine, a fleshless skeleton with its empty eye-sockets and dreadful grinning jaws.

The poor pedlar at once discovered he was on enchanted ground. The figure at the door beckoned with its fearful bony hand, and silently invited him to enter. Phil felt that if he did not instantly make his escape he would be lost for ever. He jumped up from his seat in a great hurry, and in doing so upset everything that was upon his lap—bread, meat, and with them the remains of the little pinch of SALT. No sooner did the salt touch the ground than the ghastly figure gave an unearthly yell and fell, with a noise like rattling hail, *a heap of bones.* The mighty fabric of the castle, after rocking and tottering to and fro, fell to the ground with a

THE ENCHANTED CASTLE OF BARRULL.

crash that stunned the affrighted pedlar; the air was full of cries and rushing sounds; and a dense cloud of dust rising from the ruins hid everything from his view.

He took to his heels and ran for his bare life with all his might, leaving pack, wallet, and everything behind, and, scampering straight on as fast as his legs could carry him at last emerged from the mist scared out of his wits, more dead than alive, and continued running down the mountain side till he reached the spot where Tom Kewley was standing.

When Caine had concluded his narrative, which had been most attentively listened to, not only by the Kewleys, but by several neighbours who had dropped in to hear his strange adventures, Jemmie Quine, an old man well versed in the traditions of his native land, explained that "'twas the Enchanted Castle of Barrule," and proceeded in a most oracular way to inform them all that had Phil Caine once entered into the open doorway he would never have returned, but would have been detained by the terrible magician, and the bugganes who attended him, as their slave; and further, that it was the mystic power of the salt falling to the ground which had caused the castle to collapse and disappear, and given him the opportunity of escaping.

The pedlar was housed for the night, and every one in Ballasalla took especial care in placing the usual crock of cold water at each of their cottage doors before retiring to rest, for the fairies to drink, for fear any of the wee folk or bugganes belonging to the Enchanted Castle should be passing that way in the night, and, not finding the customary offering provided for them, wreak their vengeance on the unlucky defaulters.

In the morning several of Tom Kewley's friends accompanied him and Philip Caine up the mountain road in search of the missing pack, the loss of which would have entailed ruin upon the poor bewildered pedlar. The pack was found, with its contents all safe, and beside it the wallet and scattered remnants of Philip's meal, together with his kelpie and staff.

On their return walk much talk ensued as to the dangers of the mountain road, and every one feared that for some time to come it would be unsafe to travel alone until the bugganes' anger at Philip Caine had had time to subside.

OM KEWLEY had important business at Douglas that necessitated his proceeding there a day or so after the events of the preceding chapter. A settlement between the crew of a herring-boat that he had been working with during the past season and the purchasers of their fish was to take place, and the profits of their labour divided, when the parties interested—boat-owner, master, crew, and fish-salesman—all met, and each one was paid the share due to him. This was much too serious a matter to be lightly set aside, so, spite of the entreaties of his wife and neighbours, who were sadly afraid of his falling into the hands of bugganes, or other evil-disposed fairyfolk, he made an early start to walk to Douglas.

Without any let or hindrance from either fairy or

buggane he safely reached his destination, no sign of magician's castle or aught else strange, occurring on the road; and in due course Tom Kewley received his share of the earnings of the herring-boat in the shape of good gold and silver coin. In the course of the day Tom had repeated to several small knots of friends the particulars of Philip Caine's adventure on Barrule Mountain, with all of whom he had sundry noggins. As evening drew near he prepared to set out on his return home, with his little store of money safely stowed away in the deep recesses of his breeches' pocket. With a light step and a merry heart he started, having a somewhat bulky package, slung upon his stick across his shoulder, containing various commissions he had executed for the "gude wife" at home. Just as he was passing the last houses of the town, and about to cross the old bridge at the head of the harbour, he heard his name called, and, turning round, saw Matthew Mylechreest, an old friend and shipmate, standing at the door of a house of public entertainment beckoning to him. Although he had already had as many noggins as were good for him, he could not resist Mylechreest's invitation to have a JOUGH-YN-DORIS—*anglice*, a parting glass—and another one after that, so that when he actually did make his final start, he was in that happy mellow state when all care, all fear, and all thought of the morrow is banished from the heart and brain; when the world and all about it looks cheery and good-humoured, while within there is a feeling of intense self-satisfaction, the man and himself being on the very best of terms.

By the time he parted with Mylechreest it was getting late. The sun was already down, and all folks at home were beginning to draw round their firesides, the day's work being over. Tom said a last "good-bye!" gave a last shake of the hand, and started off on his walk to Ballasalla, whistling and singing alternately as he went along; and, though he feared no robber or highwaymen, yet he kept one hand in his breeches' pocket as guard upon his bag of money, trying, as well as his somewhat muddled brain would allow him, to reckon up all that he would have to do with it, and always failing in the mental calculation as to the possibility of making twenty pounds do the work of twenty-five. Despairing after some time of being able to come to a satisfactory solution of his little sum, and having reached

THE JOUGH-YN-DORI.

the top of what is now known as Richmond Hill, he turned round and beheld Douglas town at his feet, with the lovely bay beyond.

The harvest moon was brightly shining, like a ball of burnished silver, in the heavens, shedding her soft yet brilliant light upon the dancing waves, which as they rose and fell, each one sparkling like a mass of diamonds, seemed to be clutching at the beauteous rays of the queen of night, and carrying them down into the green sea depths, far down below where corals grow and lustrous pearls lie hid. The lovely light of the moon was well set off by the deep shadows of the rocks and hills. On the extreme left, jutting boldly out to sea, stood the dark rounded head of Banks' How, with the waves breaking against its rocks in white and sparkling foam that looked like boiling silver in the light of the moon, contrasting grandly with the deep sombre head itself. On the right was the highland of Douglas Head casting a still denser gloom on the restless sea ; while in front was the town with its many glimmering lights, contrasting curiously with the effulgent beams of the harvest moon.

Although Kewley had many a time before seen the same enchanting scene, he stood some moments gazing on the beautiful panorama displayed before him, and looking first at the dancing lights upon the waves and then the cosy, comfortable lights in the houses—lights that told of many a snug fireside and jovial party assembled there. He thought he saw them all dance—lights, waves, and moonbeams—in and out, up and down, in one continuous whirl. He could not make it out ; he knew well enough it could not be that the lights actually danced, such an idea was ridiculous, so he came to the conclusion that something had disagreed with him, something indigestible, most probably it was the tanrogans—better known to Englishmen as scollops ; so in order, as he thought, to correct this and set himself to rights for his journey, he hastened on to the public-house on the hill-top, and, calling for a noggin of brandy, swallowed it down, and once more set his face towards Ballasalla.

Walking briskly down the other side of the hill he resumed his whistling and singing, each in turn, till he reached nearly to the bottom of the glen over against Mount Murray, when, during a pause in his own music, he fancied he heard another voice in the distance, singing also. He stopped, the better to listen, and far away down in the glen he heard the sounds of low, plaintive music. He proceeded on in silence, having stopped his own song, listening attentively to the other, and trying to catch the air in spite of the gentle rustling of the trees overhead. As he neared the bridge at Ballalona the sounds became louder and more distinct, and more than one voice was clearly distinguishable. He had never heard anything so charming in his life. He advanced slowly and softly, expecting every moment to come upon the serenaders and not wishing to disturb them. As he stepped upon the bridge it ceased suddenly, and then he heard at some little distance a hearty peal of laughter from many voices, mingled with sounds like the clinking of glasses and the rapping of tables. What could it be? He was quite sure no house was near. Taking a few steps, further on he stumbled over something in his path, and ere he could quite recover himself and see what it was, a voice at his feet saluted him.

"Now then, Mister Kewley! is it all the road that you're wanting? Isn't the bridge wide enough for the both of us?"

Looking down to whence the voice proceeded, he beheld a wee fairy-man standing before him. The little fellow had the most laughing eyes and rougish-looking mouth imaginable, was a compact and perfect figure, dressed in the very gayest colours, and was altogether a most gallant and pleasing, though diminutive, cavalier.

Tom, doffing his cap to the little buck, said, " Pray, sir, was it you I heard singing? I hope I have not interrupted you. I was listening so attentively I did not heed what was before me, and ask your pardon most humbly for stumbling over you.'

"*Over* me, indeed! Well, I like that certainly," replied the mannikin, whose dignity seemed offended at being considered small enough to be stumbled over, and who evidently considered himself quite as tall as Tom Kewley, whose knee was level with the feather in the fairy-man's cap.

"Oh, I beg—I beg," stammered Tom, but before he could proceed he was interrupted by the loquacious little cavalier.

" You're mighty polite, Tom Kewley! and as you seem to have brought your best manners out with you, and have a taste for music, you can come with me, and I'll introduce you to some decent society for once in your life. So follow me. But no more 'stumbling *over* me,' if you please," and

TOM KEWLEY MEETING THE LANNANSHEE.

the Lannanshee laid particular stress on the word"over," and looked very imperious; then giving Tom a knowing wink, and placing the forefinger of his right hand against the side of his nose in a most comical way, he continued, in a more friendly tone of voice—

"And if your walk has given you an appetite for supper, and the dust wants washing out of your throat, you can be well supplied with the best of good living as well as plenty of music, with drink enough to swim in ; and after refreshing yourself and putting your pipe into good tune with some liquor, the likes of which you never yet tasted, and that will very pleasantly wash all the cobwebs from your throat, you may give me and my friends the pleasure of hearing the sound of your own voice. We shall not be particular whether you sing in Manx or English; it's all one to our fraternity."

Proceeding on and talking all the while, the little elfin led Tom through a wood and over a curragh, the sounds of revelry and music becoming louder and louder at every step. Presently they emerged into an open space in front of an old ruined house, when a number of little elves, like his guide, surrounded Tom, and after playing all manner of pranks with him, pulling his coat-tails, sticking thorns into the calves of his legs, and almost tripping him up by running in front of him and between his legs, they led him down what appeared a long-standing passage into a capacious apartment with a low-groined roof like a church vault, all hung with festoons of cobwebs, upon which some of the little people were swinging.

A long and very curious shaped table was in the centre of the room, cunningly constructed of plaited fern-leaves and bullrushes, supported on innumerable mushrooms, around which were seated a large company of little ladies and gentlemen, all most gaily dressed in every conceivable variety of costume. The table was loaded with bottles, flagons, goblets, cups, and glasses of as many different shapes, sizes, and materials as the dresses of the company, and good things of all sorts were in abundance. The whole scene was one of the gayest description. Such a rollicking, merry party Tom Kewley had never seen before.

As he entered, a little lady, in a very grotesque costume, had just concluded a song, and the company were shouting their applause most vociferously and beating the table with their drinking-cups and glasses. On looking around, as he was ushered up to the further end of the room, he felt considerable surprise in recognizing in several of the little faces the features of persons he had an indistinct recollection of having seen somewhere else before, and more than one seemed to be quite familiar to him.

Feeling his coat-tail pulled and his sleeve plucked, he turned round, and seeing a little man beckoning to him to stoop down, he did so, and listened as the mannikin whispered into his ear—

" Whatever you do, Tom Kewley, don't either eat or drink anything here, or you will never return to your home in Ballasalla again. Let nothing tempt you. Beware ! "

Before Tom could ask for any explanation the little elf hurried away to his seat at the lower end of the table.

Kewley was now conducted to the presence of the fairy king, who had commanded that he should be introduced to him. This was done with much ceremony, and the little monarch received him most graciously, presenting Tom to the lovely fairy queen who sat at his left hand.

Never before had the bewildered Kewley seen anything so splendid and so beautiful as the royal pair, whose dresses were composed of the most exquisite materials, of various brilliant colours, and covered all over with bright, sparkling jewels. The queen was reserved and dignified, his small majesty was most affable and familiar, but with the air of a polished gentleman, and evidently was well used to command the respect and obedience of his rollicking and somewhat boisterous subjects.

" We welcome you, Tom Kewley, to our royal presence and to the fairy glen, for we know you well, and always find a crock of clean water standing at your door every night, and a well-swept and sanded floor on New Year's eve, when we or our queen come to Ballasalla, and my subjects give a fair report of you besides. Sit down, my good man, and join our elfin feast, for again I say you are right welcome."

Tom, who stood bowing and scraping before the royal pair, was quite overpowered by his majesty's gracious manner, and acknowledged his condescension the best way a rough countryman like him could ; and having

THE FAIRY FEAST.

been handed to a seat at the table, where room had been made for him, within good view of the royal party, he sat down, and was immediately supplied with a handsome MASSIVE SILVER CUP, which was instantly filled with wine.

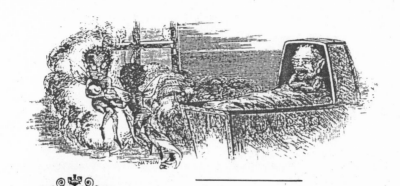

OW," said the king, so soon as his henchman had filled his jewelled goblet with bright amber-coloured wine — "now let us resume our merry-making. Let those near our mortal guest, Tom Kewley, see that he is hospitably entertained, as so worthy a guest should be, and the master of the revels can proceed to call on the next in turn for their song."

Up jumped a pretty, curly, fair-haired little elf, whose merry blue eyes proclaimed him to be full of mischief; and without any further prelude than a bow to his liege lord, and a very knowing wink as he looked towards Tom, he began the following song:

THE ELFINS' RIDE.

When wild winds howl round Snaefell's crown,
   And heavy clouds roll down his side,
We love at midnight hour to roam,
Or on a gallant steed to ride.

5

A horse we catch, of rare good stock—
No common hack will suit our taste—
A score or more will mount his back,
And round and round the fields we haste.

W J Watson

THE JADED STEED.

There's not a nag that's worth his keep
But we soon try his pace by night ;
We mount him, trot him, gallop, leap
O'er bank or stream, nought stays our flight.

On, on we ride, nor slack the speed
Till the grey east light gives warning ;

Back to his home to guide our steed,
  And hide ourselves snug ere morning.

The farmer to his farmyard hies,
  Bent on good care and feeding;
His pet nag meets his bewildered eyes
  All foam-bedecked and bleeding.

Then sure, he says, the elfin crew
  Have held their demon races;
Poor Dobbin's shaken through and through,
  Lost looks, flesh, temper, paces.

The farmer then, without delay,
  Nails on a lock to his stable door;
Makes all secure by night and day,
  Resolved we fays shall ride no more.

But we manage still to find some sport
  Where stable locks are still unknown;
And we train the pick of all the lot
  After a fashion quite our own.

"We do! we do! we do indeed!" shrieked a hundred laughing elves and bugganes, "and have our rides in spite of all."

"Bravo! bravo!" rang around the room from all sides as the singer resumed his seat.

"No one knows better than he does where to pick out a decent bit of horseflesh," said a mannikin seated next to Tom, addressing him and pointing to the singer of the last song. "And it's many a farmer that he has caused to stare in the morning when he has seen his horses, which he expected to find refreshed by their night's rest and all ready for a day's work, covered with mud and foam as if they had been galloped all over the island in the night—very likely lamed, and not fit for work for a week."

Kewley made no reply, but eyed the singer with no friendly gaze as he remembered only too sadly how sometimes his own horses had been used by the elves in much the same way.

At the bidding of the master of the revels, a very lovely little fair-haired lady now stood up, and, in the sweetest and clearest voice Tom had ever heard warbled forth the following song :

THE FAY'S SONG.

Who would not be
An airy sprite,
And lead a life of frolic gay?
From dawn till eve,
From eve till light,
We laugh the hours away.

Now 'neath the moon's
Bright silvery ray
We spread our fairy board,
Of honey sweet
On rose-leaf laid,
As fits a festal board.

The pale moon wanes,
The morn is cold,
Each fairy elf and fay,
Snug in a flower,
Enwraps herself,
To wait the broad, bright day.

From our flow'ry beds
We rise again
And bathe in the pearly dew;

Then take the air
With a butterfly pair
Link'd to a petal blue.

The evening comes.
Adown the streams,
We sail to Rushen Glen
On a lily leaf—
And meet once more
In song and dance again.

On the little Prima Donna resuming her seat she became the centre of a small select circle of admirers, all eager to lay the incense of their compliments and praises at her feet; while the uproarious applause of the rest of the rollicking assemblage made the room ring again. In the midst of the noise and confusion a party of bugganes and elves entered, tumbling over each other with most extraordinary capers and tricks, which only ceased on their being summoned into the immediate presence of the king, and ordered to give an account of their doings and the reason of their late arrival.

"Most mighty king," said one, who was the merriest and most active of the whole party, and was evidently the leader and prime mover of all their mischief and pranks, "we have been high busy, you may be sure, or we should not have been away from your gracious presence and so glorious a feast. A new-born mortal child has been changed by us to-night, and a long-standing score of vengeance paid off on that old miser Bobby Cottier, of Ballagaraghan."

"Let us hear all about it," shouted a score of voices.

"Order! order!" cried the king, flourishing his sceptre and looking as fierce as so pleasant and merry a little face could do. "You, sir, give us full particulars of the changed child first," singling out the active leader to be spokesman, "and Bobby Cottier's affair will come after."

"May it please your majesty to listen," began the merry elf, bowing with

great stateliness of body and turning his head to wink at his companions
with the most grotesque humour.   " May it please your majesty, knowing
that the wife of Paul Quiggin, of the Ballabeg Farm at Jurby, had early
yester morn had an addition to her family, we determined to steal the babe
and leave one of ourselves in its place. We commenced by drawing lots
who should be the one to be left in the cradle and be nursed by the mother
as her own child.   The lot fell on RUSTIN-WEE, whom we prepared to take
the place of the baby directly we could get a chance to make the exchange.
On arriving at Ballabeg we divided into two parties.   I, with RUSTIN-WEE
and six others, hid beneath the grass and between the stones near the door ;
while the others scampered off to the stable and cow-house, setting all the
horses and cattle loose.   They then began driving them about and making
a terrible noise, for the animals were all mad with fright, that, one after the
other, every one came running out of the house to see what was the matter
and all the disturbance about — Paul Quiggin, his brother Joe, several
others, and among them the woman who was nursing Mrs. Quiggin and the
bairn.   No sooner had they all come out, leaving Betty Quiggin and
the child alone in the house, than in we rushed, and in the twinkling of an
eye had the little one out of the cradle and RUSTIN-WEE snugly wrapped up
in his place.   Off we started, and before poor Paul and the others had got
the horses and cattle into their stalls again, we were miles away, with the
bantling, who is now safe in fairy keeping—where, you all very well know."
   "Ha! Ha! Ha!   Ho! Ho! Ho!   He! He—e !! He—e—e !!!"
burst out in chorus from every one of the elfin crew.   As for Tom
Kewley, he was frightened out of his wits at hearing of what had happened
to the Quiggins, and wished himself safe back at Ballasalla, though he
almost despaired of ever reaching there again.
   He had most rigidly heeded the warning given to him on first entering,
and had not tasted either meat or drink, though strongly pressed by his
neighbours.   Hitherto he had managed to evade their importunities ; but
could he do so much longer was very doubtful.
   " Pray what have you done to old Bobby Cottier ? " asked the king.

"Oh, not half what he deserves, your majesty. Nothing could be too bad for such a miserly old curmudgeon ; and he so seldom gives any of us a chance. The roof of his hen-roost is old ; and the stingy old beggar, grudging the cost of a little new thatch, the winds have made free with it, so that we very easily got in, sucked all the fresh eggs, and pricked all those under the setting hens. We then got through into the cow-house by shifting a loose board, which old Robby would not afford a nail on. We milked every beast quite dry ; cast an EVIL EYE on the two best cows, who will give nought but bitter milk as long as they live. Then we hied us off to the pigs, and turning the great fierce boar into the same stye with a sow and her litter of a dozen young pigs, he savagely set to and began to worry the lot ; when, the sow turning on him to defend her children, a regular scrimmage ensued. When we left, eight of the little piggies were dead—trampled to death in the fight—and the sow is so gored by her savage old lord's tusks, that the best thing Master Cottier can do in the morning will be to kill her at once to save her from dying. Just as we were coming away you could have heard the old man's shouts a mile off, for, having got up to see what the row was all about, he tumbled over a barrow standing in the doorway of his house, and broke either his shins or his head.

"Ha! Ha! Ha! Ho! Ho! Ho! He! He—e!! He—e—e!!!" shouted a host of approving bugganes.

"Serve him right if he had broken both, and his neck to boot," cried one shrill voice.

"If he had left a crock of clean water or a bowl of new milk at his door, instead of his barrow, he would have saved his shins and his pate," said another.

When the merriment at the old miser's misfortunes had somewhat subsided, and every one had made their remarks on the subject, a very important little fairy-man, who seemed by his dress and manner to be some one of great importance—a Lord Chamberlain at the very least—called every one to order, and commanded all the assembly to charge their glasses and goblets to the brim, to drink a bumper toast, and no heel-taps, to the health of their beloved royal master the great king of the Manx fairies, emperor of all elves, and lord of all bugganes.

The whole company instantly rose to their feet with brimming goblets in their hands, prepared to do full honours to the toast.

Poor Tom Kewley knew that now was the critical moment of his adventure. He feared it was all up with his ever returning to his wife and child, and was beginning to speculate in his mind how it would be possible to avoid drinking, when his eye caught sight of the same little man from whom he had received his friendly warning on entering. The little fellow was seated on the opposite side of the table some little distance off, and was gesticulating most anxiously to draw his attention and renew the caution. Tom's fears and perplexities were great indeed. If he drank, he was doomed to remain with the fairies for ever; if he refused, what vengeance would they not wreak upon him for so great an insult to their king?

He clenched his teeth in desperation, and stood up with the rest, cup in hand, and, hoping his actions would escape notice, he raised his hand and cup to his lips, and, watching his opportunity, when he thought all were too intent upon their own drinking to pay any heed to him, and had their eyes hidden in their own cups, he tilted his own over and poured the contents upon the ground.

A roar !

A most unearthly yell !

A thousand shrieks !

A most terrific peal of thunder, with a flash of lightning that seemed to burn up everything around him !

Tom Kewley saw or heard no more.

Fairies, elves, feast, and bugganes, everything vanished, and he had an indistinct feeling of being suddenly lifted up as high as the top of Snaefell, and as suddenly let fall upon the ground.

'T was some considerable time ere anything like consciousness returned to Tom Kewley, and his first supposition was
that every bone in his body was not merely broken, but
smashed into little bits, and the top of his crown utterly
crushed in by his fall. He lay on the ground for some
considerable time after consciousness did return, not daring
to open his eyes or get up, for fear the fairies would do him
further injury or kill him outright.

Hearing nothing, he ventured to open first one eye and then
the other, and raising his head a little, looked cautiously round.
He was all alone; not a creature near him but a mountain sheep
quietly grazing a few yards off. Where were all his enemies the
fairies? Had they all gone? Where was he?

He rubbed his eyes with his left hand, and sat up.

Was the whole thing a dream? No! most certainly not, for he
not only distinctly remembered all that took place, but the very

words and tunes of the songs he had heard. Looking further about him he saw several familiar sights, and after a while discovered he was in the middle of a curragh, about two miles from his own home at Ballasalla.

TOM KEWLEY AND THE CUP.

Putting his left hand into his breeches' pocket, he found to his great relief his money all safe. He had not been robbed, at any rate. It must be a

dream, then, after all. But what is this in his right hand? Nothing less
than the MASSIVE SILVER GOBLET he had used at the fairy feast, and
which he had contrived to grasp tightly in his hand amid all the uproar
and confusion attendant upon the vanishing of his elfin hosts.

No! it was no dream. The possession of the goblet proved, beyond all
doubt, it was a reality, and that he actually had been a guest at the fairy
banquet.

Tom Kewley having now proved he really was alive, not much-injured,
and in actual possession of a substantial proof of his adventure, in the
silver goblet, he lost no time in making the best of his way to Ballasalla,
where he found his wife and neighbours all in the greatest grief at his non-
appearance, and making sure he had fallen a victim to the Goblin of the
Enchanted Castle that the pedlar Philip Caine had escaped from.

After receiving the warmest of welcomes, he related to his wondering
wife and friends all the particulars of his adventure, and when he produced
his silver goblet every one was lost in astonishment. A consultation was
held as to what was best to be done with the goblet. Some doubted
whether it was silver—real silver—but the majority were in favour of its
being the true metal, and the majority was right. To keep it in the house
both he and his wife were afraid, for fear the fairies should visit them for the
purpose of reclaiming it. Several things were suggested, and amongst the
rest that the safest plan would be to take it back to the place where Tom
recovered his senses after his exit from the Fairy Hall, and leave it there for
the little people to take it away when it suited them. This was about to be
carried out, when who should pass by but Parson Gill, of Kirk Malew. He
was at once asked in and appealed to on the subject. The whole of Tom's
adventure was quickly told him, and the massive silver proof handed to him
for inspection.

The parson eyed it and weighed it well in his hand, examined it minutely,
and then, addressing his parishioners, said :

" No, my friends ! Fairies are but imps of the devil in another shape,
and when once we can get any good out of him it is folly to let him have

it back again. This cup, no doubt, is sterling right good metal, and is certainly of supernatural, and indeed I may venture to say diabolical, construction, and therefore very unfit either to be kept or used by ordinary mortal man for ordinary purposes, or even coined into current money, for it would carry a curse to every one who ever touched it. There is, however, one use, and one only, my friends, to which it can be safely, and I may venture to say appropriately, applied, and that is the services of the Church. Once safe upon the communion table, or even in the vestry cupboard, of Kirk Malew, no fairy elf or buggane in the island will ever dare attempt to remove it, or even injure or annoy the person who presented so valuable a gift to his parish church."

The parson's words were listened to with reverence and respect, and were obeyed with willingness and promptitude.

The fairies' cup was presented by Kewley to the Church, and Waldron, in his " History of the Isle of Man," mentioned that it was still in use in his time as a communion chalice, and was considered by every one as a tangible and visible proof positive, not only of the existence of fairies, but of the truth of Tom Kewley's curious adventure ; but the cup is no longer there now.

No tradition to the contrary having been ever heard, it is supposed that Tom Kewley and his family were never more molested by his elfin hosts, and that the parson was right in saying they would respect the donor of such a gift to his parish church.

King Olave the Second and the Great Sword Macabuin.

A TALE OF THE ISLE OF MAN.

KING OLAVE THE SECOND AND THE GREAT SWORD MACABUIN

N the latter part of the eleventh and the early part of the twelfth centuries, the Isle of Man was the home of the boldest race of rovers that scoured the seas; and one of the Manx monarchs, Hacon, was reckoned the mightiest sea-king of his day, and was appointed by, Edgar, king of England, to the chief command of the allied English and Manx fleets; and with three thousand six hundred vessels sailed round the British Isles and swept the seas, driving all other rovers and pirates from the face of the ocean. Well earned was his title of "Prince of Seamen," and he may be regarded as the first on the list of British admirals—a roll containing, among other proud names, the glorious ones of Drake and Frobisher, Blake and Duncan, Howe, St. Vincent, Nelson, and a host of others, the mention of whose names will ever call forth a flush of pride on a Briton's cheek.

It is of a descendant of Hacon, King Olave the Second, called Olave

Goddardson, the son of Goddard Crovan, by whom the royal sceptre of Man was for a time very worthily swayed; and the possessor of the great sword Macabuin, made by Loan Maclibhuin, the dark smith of Drontheim, our present story has to tell.

The Island of Man had some time previous been subjugated by the Norsemen, and partitioned among their several leaders or jarls, who were vassals to the king, holding their lands and possessions from him under feudal tenure; he in his turn doing homage and paying tribute to his suzerain, the king of Norway.

One of the most powerful of the many earls or jarls of Man was a

stalwart and marauding baron named Kitter, who, when not roving the seas in quest of booty, in company with other piratical Vikings, resided in an extensive but rude-built castle near the summit of South Barrule, the loftiest mountain in the southern part of the island.

ELK HORNS.[1]

In those days the inhabitants of Man were more addicted to warlike than to peaceful pursuits. Piracy was more to their taste than husbandry, and the land was wild and but poorly cultivated. The forests and moors afforded an almost undisturbed shelter for hordes of wild animals. The bison, elk, and red deer roamed over the country with other noble game,

---

[1] The above illustration is from a photograph taken from an elk's head and horns, dug up in a curragh in the south part of the Isle of Man, and are now in the possession of William Gell, Esq., of Rose Mount, Douglas.

to meet with which in these days the sportsman must cross not only the broad Atlantic, but travel far into the western wilds of America, to the slopes of the Rocky Mountains.

The chase has ever been a favourite pursuit with man in all ages, and has furnished relaxation and amusement to the greatest heroes of antiquity. Jarl Kitter, when not engaged in piratical forays on the coasts of England, Scotland, or Ireland, gave himself up to the pleasures of the chase. He was indeed a very Nimrod. Consideration for those who were peaceably inclined and cultivated the soil has never been a characteristic of mighty hunters; and in like manner to the great Norman William, king of England, and his son Rufus, who drove hundreds of poor Saxon peasants from their homes to create the great hunting-ground of the new forest in Hampshire, did this Manx jarl seek to rid the country around his domain of its human inhabitants in order the better to preserve the game.

The natural consequence was that he was both feared and hated far and wide by the peasantry. His dogs worried their cattle and flocks, while his lawless and insolent retainers damaged or destroyed their scanty crops. Many there were who only wanted the opportunity to revenge their wrongs upon the tyrant, some of whom did not hesitate to invoke the aid of witchcraft.

At a short distance from the southern coast of the Isle of Man is a smaller island, known as the Calf of Man, and Jarl Kitter's foresters, having reported to him that there were some very fine deer among the hills there, he determined to organize a great hunting expedition, and to cross over the sound which separates the Calf from the main island, and with his favourite dogs and all his retinue have a good day's sport.

He assembled all his foresters and serving-men, huntsmen and dogs to take part in the chase, leaving only his cook at home to mind the castle and prepare the feast that all would require upon their return, and set out for the Calf of Man.

Eaoch, or Loud Tongue, for so this *chef de cuisine* was named, was possessed, among other qualifications, of so surprisingly loud a voice that his

6

shout could be heard for miles, such was the extraordinary power of his lungs. He perfectly out-Stentored Stentor.

Cooking for so large a family as would assemble round the festive board on the hunting party's return was warm work.   Not only warm, but dry, so much so that Eaoch was compelled to pay frequent visits to the cellar to quench his thirst, and so much wine did he take that his culinary exertions and his potations combined, quite overpowered him, and he fell fast asleep in front of his kitchen fire.

Oda, a celebrated witch, who resided in a cavern on the coast near Port Erin, had been specially retained and feed very liberally by the suffering country people to help them in wreaking vengeance upon their common enemy, the Jarl, so soon as an opportunity should present itself.   Oda had kept a careful watch ; and directly Kitter and his retainers set forth upon their expedition, the witch took up her quarters near at hand ready to avail herself of any chance that offered itself for carrying out her purpose.

Eaoch, the cook, not only slumbered but snored ; and he did so almost as loud as he shouted.   The first grunt not only reached the watchful Oda's ear, but gave warning to the people in the country round about, that their opportunity had at last arrived.

Before he had snored many minutes Oda was by his side and saw how matters stood ; she caused a large cauldron of fat to boil over into the fire.   An instant blaze was the result, setting the whole place in flames, and some of the hot grease splashing out of the pot on to the face of Enoch, he awoke in great fright and pain.

Scalded and singed, out he rushed from the burning castle and began to roar so lustily that he gave the alarm to Jarl Kitter and his hunters on the Calf, a distance of ten miles away.

Hearing the well-known voice of his cook, the attention of Kitter was directed towards his castle, and looking in the direction of Barrule, he and his companions beheld the flames pouring forth from every door and window of the castle, and ascending with dense volumes of smoke high into the air.

The chase was instantly abandoned, and he with those of his followers who were nearest to hand, hurried down to the shore, and jumping into the first *Currach* they could reach, started to cross the narrow but rapid channel that separates the Calf from the mainland.

All was hurry and confusion; the currach itself was only a rude boat

THE LOSS OF JARL KITTER.

constructed of wicker-work covered with hides, and far too frail to combat with the surging, boisterous waters of the Sound, as the channel is called, which were rushing through the narrow space between the two islands like a mill race.

Oda, the witch, guessing that Kitter's party could not fail to be alarmed at the sound of Eaoch's shouts and the smoke from the burning castle, would return as soon as possible, hastened down to the south shore, and standing on the top of the high, precipitous rock now known as Spanish Head,[1] watched the embarkation of the Jarl and his hunters in the currach.

Using her powers of witchcraft, she speedily caused a storm to arise. The boat was overcrowded and unsteady. Jarl Kitter swore worse than any Flanders trooper, the helmsman's wonted skill forsook him, and he with his shipmates became panic-struck at the sudden storm.

The rapid current and the wind together drove the fragile and over-burdened vessel violently upon a rocky islet lying midway between the two shores. She at once swamped and capsized, leaving every one of its living freight struggling in the raging sea. It was in vain to cling to the rocks and call for help. The waters overwhelmed them all, and washed them one by one into the surging stream. All perished, not a soul was saved.

The rocky islet has ever since that day, in commemoration of this event, borne the name of Kitterland, or Kitter's Island.

[1] This headland is so called in consequence of a large ship of the Spanish Armada being wrecked there, after trying to escape from one of Drake's vessels that had chased her right round the north of Scotland.

HE other jarls of Man, hearing of the fate of their friend and neighbour Kitter, and fearing a general rising of the Manx peasantry against them, assembled together to take counsel for their united defence. Their suspicions were unanimously fixed on Eaoch, the cook, who they believed had purposely been the cause of his master's death, and of being in league with the country people to destroy or drive from the island all the nobles of Norwegian descent.

He had been arrested almost immediately, and was accused before King Olave Goddardson, who, being a just man, ordered him to be brought face to face with his accusers. Great preparations were made for the trial the king commanded should be held. The jarls took good care that the jury should consist exclusively of their own order, and though King Olave did all in his power to secure him a fair hearing, Eaoch met with but scant justice. A speedy conviction resulted, and sentence of death was pronounced. The cook heard his sentence with perfect composure, and so soon as it was pronounced he claimed the privilege then allowed by both Norwegian and Manx law to all native born subjects condemned to death, of choosing the place and manner of his own execution.

His application was granted by his royal judge as a matter of course, and cn hearing the king's consent to his request the condemned cook exclaimed :

" The death I choose is this. I will place my head on one of your majesty's legs, and it shall there be cut off with your majesty's great sword MACABUIN, which was made by LOAN MACLIBHUIN, the dark smith of Drontheim."

On hearing this every one was horror-struck, for they saw in a moment the cunning of the varlet, who knew full well the magic properties of the great sword, and calculated on the king's refusal to run so great a risk of losing his leg and most likely his life.

Every one, nobles and common people alike, begged and prayed of the king to refuse the prisoner's preposterous request, the compliance with which would be placing himself in such imminent danger, for the powers and properties of the great sword were very terrible.

The great sword, MACABUIN, had been made specially for King Olave by LOAN MACLIBHUIN, the dark smith of Drontheim, assisted by fairies and bugganes, who superintended its forging and tempering. It would sever anything and everything its edge was brought in contact with, even solid iron or granite rock, and when once it began to cut, there was no knowing where it would stop. When he first received this wonderful sword King Olave was bade to try its powers, and being at the time encamped between Douglas and Laxey he struck two huge stones one after the other and clave them in twain. There the stones stand to this day, where they may be seer. near the roadside, and are pointed out to the visitors when going from

Douglas to see the great wheel of Laxey Mines. It is said of these stones that whenever they hear the cock crow at sunrise they clap together with a great noise.

THE WITCHES' CONCLAVE.

Knowing the wondrous properties of this sword, no wonder all the people, with whom the king was very popular and much beloved, dreaded the effects of carrying out the cook's request, and fearing for his majesty's safety, begged of him not to submit to it.

There was no compromise possible in the matter. Either the king must run this terrible risk of having his leg cut off, or the condemned man be liberated.

Olave Goddardson was a true knight, and his word once given nothing could induce him to forfeit it. In spite of bishops and priests offering him indulgence and absolution, he insisted on keeping his plighted word to the condemned varlet, Eaoch, and no inducement could prevail upon him to do aught derogatory to his fair fame as a man and a king.

The preparations for Eaoch's execution were therefore proceeded with, the whole island bewailing what was considered must necessarily result in the death of their beloved king.

With a view if possible of overcoming the terrible cutting properties of the great sword all the witches in the island were consulted, and they held a midnight meeting at the full of the moon on the summit of Snaefell, the highest mountain in the island.

Their weird consultations were presided over by Oda, the very crone who had caused all the mischief by making the pot of fat boil over, and so setting fire to Jarl Kitter's castle.

After much discussion among the ancient wise ladies, and consulting of many mystic records, together with the working of several incantations, a charm was at last decided upon and prepared, to be placed on the Royal Leg, prior to the condemned cook laying his head upon this extraordinary block of his own selection.

It was only at the urgent solicitations and prayers of his subjects that the king consented to allow the charm to be used.

TOADSKINS, flayed from the reptiles alive ;

TWIGS OF THE ROWAN TREE,[1] twisted round and bound together with GREY HAIRS plucked from the CHINS of MAIDEN WOMEN, and

ADDERS' EGGS.

Each to the number of nine times nine were skilfully amalgamated

---

[1] The rowan is the ash tree.

tcgether, and cunningly formed into a pad or cushion of seven times seven layers.

The day fixed upon for the execution of Eaoch the cook at length arrived, and an immense concourse of people assembled from all parts of the Isle of Man at the TYNWALD MOUNT, the spot where all public ceremonials took place, and where, at the present day, Her Majesty Queen Victoria's representative presides at the proclamation of the Manx laws that have been passed during the past session of the House of Keys—the insular parliament —and on her behalf he gives the royal assent to the same once every year—the first Monday in July, which is kept as a general holiday. [1] All the preparations being completed for the execution, the charm was produced, and with much ceremony and

THE WITCHES' CHARM.

[1] The Tynwald Hill is a mound of earth composed of ground brought from every parish in the island, and is situated on the roadside at St. John's, as near as possible in the centre of the island. It has been used for these purposes from time immemorial, and gives its name to the highest court of law in the island, the Court of Tynwald, which is presided over by the Lieutenant-Governor in person.

many mystic rites, carefully bound on the king's leg by the arch-witch Oda herself. The assembled people looked on in eager-suspense, and the deepest anxiety was depicted on every face. The culprit having been previously shriven, was led forth to his doom. His appearance was the signal for a perfect storm of yells and execrations from the crowd. He was seized by two stalwart Norsemen, and after being blindfolded, was led up to the royal chair, where he was bid to kneel and lay his head upon what he had himself so cunningly elected as the block—the leg of King Olave. One of the king's body-guard, named Ulrid, a veteran renowned in many a hard-contested fight for his undaunted courage, his great strength, and his peculiar steadiness of hand and nerve, was selected for executioner.

The mighty and terrible sword Macabuin, made by Loan Maclibhuin, the dark smith of Drontheim, was brought forth from the king's armoury by two other guardsmen, and laid with great state and ceremony before the throne. On drawing it forth from its sheath, its bright and polished blade reflected back the brilliant rays of the midday sun, glittering and flashing like a sword of fire, dazzling the eyes of all beholders. Lifting up the sword with the greatest caution, and bracing every nerve of his powerful and brawny arms, in order to keep its destructive powers well in check, he laid its edge gently upon the neck of Eaoch.

Not a sound was heard. All the vast multitude looked on in silence and with bated breath, terribly anxious for the result of the magic charm, which alone could counteract the fearful powers of the dreadful sword, and stay its descent before reaching the brave king's leg.

Great was the trepidation of the whole assembled court on beholding that even the strong and steady hand of the king's most trusty guardsman could not stay the onward and downward progress of the wondrous weapon, when once its edge began to cut.

The sword Macabuin made but short work of the neck of Eaoch, severing it clean from his body, without a single hitch or hesitation on passing through the bone. Straight through it went ; and, much to the horror of

THE EXECUTION OF EAOCH THE COOK.

those near the king, it continued still to cut, in spite of the efforts of the guardsman to restrain its progress, dividing asunder slowly, but steadily and surely, layer after layer of the preventive charm, till it reached the very last grey maiden's hair, and then it stopped. The spell was broken, and the magic power of the great sword Macabuin was at an end. The executioner once again had a perfect control over the weapon, and lifting it up from the royal leg, which had not received the slightest injury, he waved the blood-stained blade triumphantly around his head.

Great was the joy and loud the shouts (almost as loud as those of the dead cook's) of every one when they saw the success of the potent charm, and that their beloved king remained uninjured. Fires were speedily kindled on the mountain tops, and from hill to hill the joyful news was spread throughout the whole length and breadth of the island, "The king is saved," "Long live the king!"

Olave jumped up directly the executioner had lifted up the sword from his leg, and kicked the ghastly bleeding head on one side. He then proceeded in solemn procession, attended by all his court and thousands of his assembled people, to Peel, and entering the cathedral of St. Germain's, returned thanks, and offered many precious gifts at the shrine of that saint in gratitude for his wonderful preservation.

AOCH'S extraordinary execution, with the particulars of King Olave's steadfast courage and escape, soon became the topic of conversation far and wide, and was the theme of many a travelling minstrel's song. In time the news reached the shores of Norway and the city of Drontheim, where it came at last to the ears of Loan Maclibhuin, the swarthy smith of that ilk.

When he heard of the stratagem and weird device adopted by the Manx witches, and submitted to by the king to thwart the efficacy of his *chef d'œuvre*, the great sword Macabuin, he stormed and raged with frantic fury, uttering curses and denunciations on the king, on the witches, and on the whole Manx people. He summoned his confidential servant and chief hammerman, an old cripple named HIALLUS-NAN-URD, and bid him start at once to the Isle of Man, and go to the court of King Olave Goddardson, at Peel Castle, with a message he imparted to him in secret.

Hiallus-nan-urd had only one leg, having lost the other in the service of his master while assisting that wonderful smith in the manufacture of the great sword Macabuin.   Swords, however, were not the only articles manufactured in the Drontheim smithy, and Loan Maclibhuin had cunningly contrived for his crippled servant an artificial limb, which, though not worked either by steam or clockwork and springs, like the leg of Mynheer von Clam, was a very curious piece of mechanism, and, unlike that of the Dutchman, though it " never got tired," was under the perfect control of its owner.

The hammerman started off, and in due time reached Peel Castle, where he demanded to be admitted to an audience with his Majesty of Man.   On being ushered into the royal presence, he then and there taunted the king with unknightly conduct in having offered insult to his own good sword— the great sword Macabuin, which had been made expressly for and presented to him by the dark smith, Loan Maclibhuin of Drontheim, and he concluded with challenging the king to walk with him from Peel Castle to the smithy at Drontheim.

Such a challenge, publicly given before his whole court, coupled with so grave an accusation, could not be refused without ineffable disgrace and a total loss of caste.   The honour of Olave Goddardson was at stake, and he had no alternative but to accept the challenge of the offended Loan Maclibhuin.   This he did in spite of a solemn warning given to him by Oda the witch, who, scenting the arrival of the strange one-legged ambassador from Norway, and auguring no good from his visit, had hastened to the court at Peel Castle, and was present at the meeting between him and the king.

She privately informed Olave Goddardson that the challenge was only a ruse to decoy him to his destruction, for the dark smith was at that very time engaged upon the construction of another magic sword, which was to possess even more wonderful powers than the once celebrated, but now dishonoured, Macabuin, in his Majesty's possession.   She also informed him that news had been brought to her by a raven, with three white spots on its breast, that had arrived the night previous direct from Norway, of its having been prophesied by Haco-Norjid, a noted wizard of that country, that the new sword now being made by Loan Maclibhuin, the dark smith of Drontheim, would be a wonderful success, and possessed of supernatural and invincible powers far beyond that of Macabuin, or of any other weapon ever yet produced in the world ; but that in order to insure this success it was necessary that the steel should be tempered in live royal blood.

Oda at once divined that it was the dark smith's intention to entrap King Olave Goddardson into visiting his smithy at Drontheim for the sole purpose of making him the victim whose royal blood should give the required temper and miraculous powers to the great sword he was now engaged upon.

On hearing Oda's communication the king thanked her for the warning, but told her it was too late to withdraw from the challenge.

Followed by the good wishes and prayers of all his people, King Olave started off on his journey to walk with Hiallus-nan-urd, the one-legged hammerman of Loan Maclibhuin, from Peel Castle to the smithy at Drontheim. No sooner had they started than a large black raven, with three white spots upon its breast, was seen to rise into the air, and, after three flights round the towers of Peel Castle, to take the same course as the travellers, keeping steadily over the king's head. Oda, the Manx witch, was determined that King Olave should, in case of need, receive due warning of any danger or treachery that might threaten his safety while away, and that raven was intrusted by her with a special mission for that purpose, with strict instructions ever to keep a close watch on the one-legged hammerman, and on no account to allow him to arrive at the smithy at Drontheim before the king.

ING OLAVE and the one-legged hammerman journeyed on
day after day, neither one gaining much advantage over the
other. They both reached the Point of Ayre, the northern-
most coast of the Isle of Man, the day after leaving Peel
Castle. Here each had a boat in readiness to cross the
narrow sea to the neighbouring shores of Scotland, and on
landing there they both started off again on their pedestrian
race to cross the land of the Thistle to the north-eastern coast,
where they hoped to find vessels to convey them over the sea
to Norway.

Ever near the king, flying over his head by day and roosting near his
pillow at night, the faithful raven kept constant watch. The Norwegian
land was at last reached, and then commenced the real race, each of them
being eager to be the first to enter the smithy of Loan Maclibhuin at
Drontheim. So close did they keep together that, on arriving within sight
of their destination, they were neck and neck.

Now was the time for the sable bird to do the king a good service.
This he did by adroitly and unseen dropping a small but very sharp pebble
into the one shoe of Hiallus-nan-urd, which, getting under his foot, caused
him great pain, and to limp worse than he did before on account of his

artificial leg. The hammerman was compelled to stop and take off his shoe to remove the pebble, while the king made a vigorous effort and pushed forward rapidly, the raven having whispered into the king's ear. Olave Goddardson's increased speed enabled him to leave the hammerman behind some distance, and to enter the smithy of Loan Maclibhuin before his competitor. On entering he closed the door behind him, much to the surprise and chagrin of the swarthy smith, who recognized him at once. Without taking any notice of Loan Maclibhuin, the king determined to show that he was not distressed or tired by the fatigues of his long and hurried journey, seized hold of a huge sledge-hammer, and swinging it round his head, struck it with such force upon the anvil that he clove the massive block of iron in twain, and shivered the stone bed, upon which it rested, into pieces.

The wizard-smith looked out eagerly to see if his ally and messenger, Hiallus-nan-urd, was near at hand, when Olave, hearing the ominous croaking of his attendant raven, suddenly bethought him of the witch's warning that the challenge was a mere ruse to decoy him there for his destruction, looked round for any signs of the great sword he knew Loan Maclibhuin was engaged in making, and which he was convinced must be somewhere near at hand. On casting his eyes towards the fire he beheld what he sought ; and walking boldly across the smithy he seized it in his hand, greatly to the dark smith's confusion and amazement.

At the same moment that the king had entered, a door at the side of the smithy, and placed considerably in the shade, might have been seen to open, and from it had entered, unseen by him, a Norwegian maiden of surpassing fairness and beauty, who was a witness of his prowess with the sledge-hammer and the anvil. She advanced into the light as the king had laid his hand upon the great sword, when, for the first time, he perceived her and was immediately struck with her beauty.

Hearing the stumping of the artificial leg of the hammerman drawing near to the door outside, and being again reminded by the croaking of the faithful raven, which began now to flap his wings in great impatience, and

7

peck at the king's feet, he had but little time for compliments or admiration ; so, addressing himself to the maiden, and pointing with his left hand to the dark smith, he said, " Say, fair maid, is not this your father, Loan Maclibhuin, the seventh son of old Windy Cap, king of Norway? "

" He is, Sir knight," replied Emergaid, for so was the beauteous daughter of the royal blacksmith named.

" Then ! " exclaimed the king of Man, drawing forth the red-hot steel from the fire before either the smith or his hammerman, who was now about to enter, had time to prevent him—" then thus do I fulfil the wizard's prophecy ! Your blood, old man, is royal blood like my own, and in royal living blood shall this good blade be tempered."

With his left arm he gently pushed aside the fair Emergaid, who had stepped forward to protect her father, and springing towards him, plunged the red-hot sword into the old smith's heart.

" And," continued King Olave, withdrawing the hissing blade from the body as it fell at his daughter's feet, and turning towards the door, "thus do I punish you my one-legged travelling companion, and prove the temper of this wondrous sword."

Before the now affrighted Hiallus-nan-urd could reach the door again to make his escape, the king made one cut at him, and, striking on the top of his head, the sword went down through his body, severing it in two.

No sooner had the divided hammerman fallen to the ground than the white-spotted raven pounced upon one half. Seizing the still quivering heart, he tore it out, and flew off with it in the direction of the Isle of Man, croaking quite triumphantly as he passed out of the open window.

The fair Emergaid had swooned directly she saw her father fall, and thus was spared the dreadful sight of the hammerman's fate.

To her the twice-saved monarch now turned his attention, and raising her gently in his arms, he bore her from the smithy, gazing with admiration on her lovely face. As he did so he felt his own heart struck by as hot and sharp a pang as that by which he had slain her father.

        *   *   *   *   *   *

THE DEATH OF LOAN MACLIBHUIN, THE DARK SMITH.

At first the wooing of King Olave Goddardson did not progress. Grief for the loss of her father forbade her listening to the love of him who had made her an orphan. Still her first sight of him, when he proved how stalwart a knight he was by cleaving her father's anvil, had more than favourably impressed her, and she could not but admire so gallant a suitor ; so as he was as resolute in love as in other matters, he finally won her consent and made the best amends he possibly could for depriving her of one protector in her father by becoming himself her protector and her husband.

Suffice to say that his frank and manly bearing won her heart, and she consented to share with him the royal honours and duties of his little island kingdom.

King Olave conducted his lovely bride with a large fleet in great state to the Isle of Man, where he had her crowned queen ; and though history is silent on the subject, we may naturally conclude they lived happily together.

From the union were descended a long line of kings of Man, one of whom was the great Olave the Black, the boldest sea rover of his day. The last descendants of Olave Goddardson and Emergaid the Fair, who reigned in Mona, was Magnus, and in him ended the royal race of Goddard Crovan, surnamed the Conqueror.

The Buggane's Vow:

A LEGEND OF ST. TRINION'S CHURCH.

ERY many years ago, during the period when that redoubt-
able warrior William the Norman was following up his successful battle of Hastings, and making good his possession
of the good land of England, there was a certain Irish chief-
tain named BRODAR MERUNE, who, being a regular "broth
of a boy," fond of the best of good living, and keeping open
house, found himself, at the period of our story, like many
more of his hospitable and improvident countrymen of
these degenerate days, a trifle short of cash ; and it being
long prior to the invention of loan societies, limited banks,
or even bill-stamps, he had none of the facilities for obtaining accommodation or "flying a kite" that are now enjoyed by his descendants.

Money, however, Brodar Merune must have by some means or other,
for his needs were pressing, so going to his strong chest, he brought forth
the family jewels—real Irish diamonds—and determined on them to nego-
tiate a loan. But, unfortunately, none of his countrymen were in a position
to assist him ; every one was as hard up as he was himself. Among his
retainers was one Crorty, who had frequently visited the neighbouring
Island of Man when engaged in fishing expeditions, and he informed his

master that at the foot of Grebah Mountain, not very far from the port of Peel in that island, there resided a rich old curmudgeon of a jarl named Haco, who, not being possessed of the same amount of personal courage and daring as his brother nobles, thought it better to remain quietly at home when they went forth on their marauding and piratical expeditions. Jarl Haco, though fond of quiet and of a timorous disposition, was, if not *hot*-headed, very *long*-headed, and the talents that his neighbours employed in planning and carrying out predatory expeditions to the neighbouring coasts of England and Wales, he devoted to mercantile matters, and as he was careful, cunning, and a smart man of business, he soon became the richest man in Ellan Vannin.

Always ready to lend his more valiant and pugnacious friends money when they required the sinews of war for the fitting out of some fresh foray— taking good care always to have ample security in hand—Jarl Haco, of Grebah Castle, was, in fact, an *Attenboronian* baron—a mediæval money-lender.

On hearing of the Lord of Grebah, Brodar Merune determined to take his family jewels and set sail for the Isle of Man, for the purpose of obtaining a supply of the necessary means of keeping open house a little longer, by raising a loan. The winds were propitious, and he soon arrived at Peel, where he landed without delay, and set forth in quest of Jarl Haco, who he found at his castle at the foot of Grebah Mountain. He showed him a specimen of the glittering jewels, and had no difficulty in coming to terms for the much-required advance, being, like many others in a similar strait, not over particular as to conditions so long as he could actually get the cash.

It was agreed that Jarl Haco should send down the sum required by one of his own servants to the ship of Brodar Merune at Peel, where, on receiving from him the remainder of the jewels, he was to hand over the bags of coin.

On arriving at Peel with the money in his possession, Jarl Haco's messenger, Quiggar by name, proceeded to the vessel of the Irish baron who, seeing that he was alone (for the old Manx money-lender had not for one moment suspected treachery on the part of his Celtic client), was sudder.ly tempted to try and possess himself of the money without parting with his family jewels. Inviting the messenger on board, he very obsequiously handed him down into the cabin, and bidding the attendants bring refreshments, the table was soon laden with flagons, cups, and all the concomitants for brewing *potteen*.

"Are ye dhry?" said Brodar Merune, giving the messenger a seat and helping to place the money-bags on the cabin table. "Sit down, man, and be asy. It's time enough to do business when ye've washed your throat and got breath, for it's a smart bit of a walk ye have had, and carrying thim heavy bags too. Here, boy! be sharp now and bring the hot wather, and mind it boils. Don't ye see the gentleman's exhausted with fatague? and well he may be, carrying such a weight on him. All goold too. Sure it's lucky the folks are honest in these parts, or ye might have had throuble on the road. Faith! ye would in my counthry if it was known what it was ye were carrying."

It was not long before a jorum of hot strong whiskey-punch was brewed and placed before the Baron and his guest, who enjoyed it famously, for it was but little of the good things of this life he ever saw or tasted at Grebah Castle.

Brodar Merune, who had a hard and well-seasoned head himself, and could drink enough to wash a horse, saw that his guest's bowl was frequently replenished, and after a little time produced the jewels and proposed to count out the contents of the money-bags.

The table was soon covered with little piles of coin and the Irish diamonds, which latter shone and sparkled most brilliantly, like twinkling stars of the first magnitude, before the eyes of the unwary Manxman, who was emptying his goblet as fast as it was replenished, for the liquor was good.

By the time the fifth brewing was disposed of, the gold and the jewels all seemed to be dancing on the board together, and Quiggar found it difficult to distinguish which was which. He had long since lost all count of the reckoning, as the Baron told over and piled up the golden coins before him, till at length, being completely overpowered with the too seductive liquor, his head fell forward on his bosom, and presently a loud snorting snore informed his host that the potteen had done its work.

THE EFFECTS OF POTTEEN.

Calling several of his crew he bid them carefully carry the prostrate Quiggar upon deck, and, hoisting him over the side, they laid him comfortably in a snug place on the shore, when Brodar gave orders to prepare for immediate departure.

The vessel had been lying for some days in Peel Harbour while Brodar Merune was negotiating his business with the Jarl of Grebah, and the crew had been engaged in refitting and setting up the rigging and other repairs requisite to be done in port. Such was now the hurry to get the ship to sea, with the money Brodar Merune had so dishonestly secured before Jarl Haco's messenger could recover from his drunken fit and get to his master with the news of his loss, or obtain assistance from his countrymen in Peel to stop the vessel's departure, that neither he nor his companions had paid any heed to the warning given to them by some of the crew of a Manx ship laying alongside, who told them to kindle a fire and carry a burning brand all over the vessel to drive out the fairies, bugganes, witches, and other spirits that may be hidden on board before sailing, and which could only be done by fresh kindled fire and while the ship was still in contact with the shore. Such has been, and is indeed now, the custom with Manx sailors and fishermen from time immemorial.

Brodar Merune just then heeded nothing of fairies, witches, or bugganes, and thought only of making off as quickly as he could with the money-bags of the Jarl of Grebah, which he had so cleverly, as he thought, succeeded in getting possession of.

The anxiety of Brodar Merune to get to his own country across the sea was so great, he could pay no attention to anything but getting his vessel under weigh, and his only thought was to hurry on his departure.

Chap. II

PEEL Harbour once cleared, all sail was set on to the vessel, and as the evening closed in she was well away from the land of Mona, making a fair way towards the Irish coast—Brodar Merune pacing the deck, and chuckling to himself as he contemplated his cleverness in· overreaching the commercial Manxman and called to mind his poor drunken messenger.

The moon in due time began to rise, and so did the wind and the sea ; and just as the last rays of the setting sun dipped below the western horizon with a lurid flush that should have been a warning to mariners to prepare for a dirty night, a little buggane, who had got on board at Peel and had been asleep all day, now woke up and cautiously crept on deck. When the little elf discovered that he was no longer lying quietly in Peel Harbour, but that all sail was set and the vessel bounding merrily over the fast-rising waves, he essayed to give a look about him, and discovered it was no Manx fishing-boat he was on board of, but an over-sea bound barque, and he was being fast carried away from his own beloved Ellan Vannin.

He had no notion of being taken to he knew not where, and leaving all his own haunts and companions behind, so he straightway ran to the end of the vessel's bowsprit, and set to work vigorously to blow her back towards the point she had just left. His labours resulted in changing the direction of the wind and increasing its violence ; and, much to his annoyance, Brodar Merune found his ship taken flat aback, and a stiff gale of wind blowing in just the contrary direction to which he desired to go.

The Irish baron was no chicken-hearted fellow, to give in to what he called a mere squall; so, calling all hands on deck, he ordered the sails to be trimmed, the yards braced sharp up, and proceeded to beat against the wind, tack and tack, persisting on his course westward, and endeavouring to make the best of his way to his native land.

The buggane, enraged at the perseverance of the baron and his crew, redoubled his own efforts, blowing all the harder. More reefs were taken in, everything made secure, and two of the most experienced men in the ship placed at the helm, with orders to keep her head as close up to the wind as possible; and the vessel beat up on her homeward course.

The buggane was only the more determined to have his own way when he saw the redoubled efforts of the Irishmen ; so as the ship was tacking and coming round, the imp of mischief caused one of the masts to snap close off by the deck just at the critical moment of going about. The wreck of the mast fell over the side and beat heavily against the labouring vessel, and before the crew could cut away the wreck a butt was started, and the water commenced to pour into the hold. The pumps were rigged, and part of the crew told off to work them ; but with only one mast and a leaky ship the baron and his crew were forced to give in, and abandoning all idea of reaching the Irish coast, thought only of running into a safe haven in the Isle of Man and so saving their lives.

The order to " 'Bout ship!" was given, and making the most of their remaining mast and sail, the vessel's head was laid on a course direct for the island, and she scudded before the gale.

The weather, far from moderating, got worse and worse. The leak increased upon the pumps, which were of the very rudest description, and as they neared the rugged, rocky coast of the Isle of Man their dangers increased, and the chance of safety became less and less.

The mischievous little buggane, not satisfied with having compelled Brodar Merune to abandon his voyage and return to the port he sailed from, now directed his efforts to the total destruction of the ship and crew, and for this purpose guided her course straight towards the bluff, rocky coast of Contrary Head, some little distance south of Peel Harbour, between there and Port Erin.

Success turned the little elfin's head. He capered about in high glee as he contemplated the results of his diabolical efforts, and when he saw that the poor storm-tossed barque was being hurriedly driven against the surf-lashed rocks, towering five hundred feet above their heads, he danced and crowed and chuckled with fiendish delight, and skipped about all over the ship, gleefully clapping his little hands together in the most ecstatic manner.

Suddenly the idea occurred to him that, to make his work quite sure, he had better unship the rudder, and thus render the vessel utterly helpless; and he was just about to carry it into execution, when suddenly he felt a curious and rather disagreeable sensation. He became aware of the presence of a superior and controlling influence, a something antagonistic to himself. The little creature felt all his power and his courage oozing gradually away.

The ship's head slowly but steadily diverged from the course he had been directing it on to the rocks, and the crew taking advantage of a slant of wind off shore, she was now fast escaping the destruction to which he had doomed her and the hapless crew.

What could it all mean ! He looked cautiously round to ascertain what.

could possibly have brought all his exertions to nought. Lo! there beside the companion leading into the cabin was Brodar Merune on his knees on the deck, his head uncovered, and holding before him a small leaden image of Saint Trinion, which seemed to glow with a pale light of glory. To this sainted bishop of the ancient Picts was Brodar Merune praying most fervently to save him and his crew.

The buggane's limbs trembled and shook as he looked on, awe-struck and aghast, at the kneeling baron pouring forth his prayers.

"Oh, blessed Saint Trinion! sure it's a moighty fine job, it is, that I had ye in my pouch : it's lost entirely we should be, every mother's son of us. Oh, blessed bishop! only just see if ye can't save us this once, and I'll return the Manxman all his dirty money, ivery groat of it ; and I'll build a most illigant church for your own blessed holiness yourself—faith I will."

Here the wind apparently increased in violence, and the ship seemed to leap nearer still to the frowning rocks. These signs Brodar took as an evidence that the holy man doubted the sincerity of his promise.

"Och! sure indade but I will, honour bright. And I'll build it *as far from this blackguard say as I can find a spot* dhirectly I get safe and sound on dhry land once again. Oh, indade but I will, and return ould Haco all his purty bright goold again ; and, faith, it's sell him my own darlint bright jewels, I will, and spend the whole of the money on the church for ye, that I will, sure enough, oh, most holy Saint Trinion! if ye will only make haste and save us all out of this."

No sooner had this petition and vow been uttered, than the saint hastened to the rescue. The first thing he did was to alter the ship's course, so that she could clear the rocks. He then stopped the leak by causing some seaweed to drift into the open seam, and looking round to see what else required attention, he espied, crouching down by the side of the broken mast, the now no longer triumphant, but shivering and frightened little buggane. Stepping up to where he was, the saint seized him between his holy finger and thumb by the scruff of his neck, and pitched him high up on to the top of the cliff that had so lately loomed down upon the battered ship, as if ready to fall upon and crush her and the worn-out crew.

The little sprite quickly recovered his feet, and rubbing his sore bones, turned round savagely to spit his puny spite at the ship and her guardian saint, deeply vowing vengeance as he watched, with manifest chagrin, the vessel, safely guided by Saint Trinion, make her way into Peel harbour. He stamped and danced with rage, and vowed to be even with the bishop. Had he been educated at the Vatican he could not have uttered his anathemas in more approved style, and his language was far from being either parliamentary or polite. He wound up by vowing most solemnly that "SAINT TRINION SHOULD NEVER HAVE A WHOLE CHURCH IN ELLAN VANNIN."

Safely landed, the penitent Baron Brodar Merune, true to his promise —unlike many people who make vows when in distress but forget them— hurried off to Jarl Haco's castle at Grebah, where he found the money-lending noble deeply deploring the loss of his beloved gold, and highly exasperated against his luckless messenger for being so fooled out of his treasure. The poor fellow Quiggar was locked up in the lowest dungeon of the castle, loaded with chains, fetters, and all the other uncomfortable appliances used in those days to add to the horrors of imprisonment. Haco was like many others both before and since his time, who are but too glad to find some one on whom to wreck their vexed and angered feelings. He was just then debating in his own mind how he should put the poor wretch to death, so as to give him the most pain and suffering and himself the greatest amount of satisfaction for the loss of his bright golden pieces.

When first the shock-headed retainer who did duty at Grebah Castle as head footman announced Brodar Merune, and that repentant baron entered, carrying in one hand his family jewels and in the other the heavy bags of gold, the old Jarl thought it must be the ghost of the man who had wronged him, or that he must surely be dreaming. When, however, Brodar Merune laid down the bags on the table one by one, and his ears caught the delightful sound of the peculiar chink of the gold coins in the bags, which was delicious music to Jarl Haco, he stared with astonishment.

"Here, friend Haco," said the baron, as he deposited the last bag of coin on the floor, "here is your money back, every piece—every groat of the sum your messenger brought me."

"Can it be possible?" murmured the Jarl.

Brodar Merune soon convinced him it was quite possible, and that not only had he come to restore the lord of Grebah Castle his gold, but had brought his jewels, all of them, to sell outright.

Haco on hearing this felt a change come over himself, and brightened up at once. He was ready for business immediately, and only too eager to hear the proposal Brodar had to make, fully prepared to take every advantage he possibly could of the uncommercial Irishman; for he felt convinced that something more than common must have happened to have caused such a man as he was to restore what he had once possessed himself of, either by fair means or foul. Brodar Merune proceeded to relate all the particulars of his adventures to the attentive Haco, glossing over, in the best way he could, the ugly fact of his making the luckless Quiggar drunk, and then turning him on shore without either money or diamonds.

He fully described all the horrors of the storm, with their forlorn condition, and narrow escape through the timely arrival of the blessed Saint Trinion, who had come in answer to his prayers. He then proceeded to inform Jarl Haco that he had vowed most solemnly to devote the proceeds of his jewels to the building a church in the Isle of Man, as far from the sea as he could find a suitable spot. The church was to be dedicated to the holy Saint Trinion, Bishop of the Picts, who had signally saved him and all his comrades from a watery grave.

The old Jarl listened attentively, and pricked up his ears when told where the church was to be built. He had a keen eye to business, and, ever ready to seize an opportunity for a bargain, at once informed his visitor that he knew of a very eligible spot for the intended church, as

BRODAR MERUNE RESTORING THE MONEY.

near as possible in the very centre of the Isle of Man, and not very far from where they were now sitting. It was on some land forming part of a farm that was mortgaged to him by a poor farmer, and as he was in arrears with his payments of interest, he should give orders to foreclose at once, and take possession of the property. The spot selected was as nearly as possible the very centre of the island, and therefore exactly suited to the purpose of building a church, which must be in compliance with the terms of Brodar Merune's vow, "*as far from the blackguard sea as possible;*" and as they were going to do business, the land for the church could go as part payment for the diamonds. A price was soon fixed and agreed upon for the jewels and also for the land.

DESIGN for the church was settled, which those who are acquainted with the primitive barn-like simplicity of the ecclesiastical architecture of the Isle of Man will readily understand did not occupy much time in doing. The work was commenced without delay. Jarl Haco very liberally gave the stone for the building the church for nothing, pointing out a spot on his property from which it was to be quarried by the baron's men. Curiously enough, the old Jarl had long been wanting some rugged rocks cleared away from that spot, to carry out some improvements he wished to make, but he begrudged the expense. How very lucky some people are in being able to make the carrying out of their own selfish purposes and designs bear the appearance of an act of charity. He furthermore promised to present to the church a stained-glass window, which he intended should bear his own name, be a memorial of his own glorification, and he quite anticipated the pleasure he should experience in contemplating his own munificent gift when seated in the church.

Many were the difficulties the builders of this church had to contend against in its construction, for the vicious little buggane had not forgotten either his bruises, when Saint Trinion pitched him neck and crop out of the Irish baron's ship on to the rocks, and disappointed him of his intention of wrecking the vessel, or of the oath he had sworn that " *The sainted bishop should never have a whole church in Ellan Vannin.*"

All the vengeful little elf could do to thwart the efforts of the workmen he did. The horses that drew the stone from the quarry were lamed in various ways. The quarrymen were continually being hurt by stones falling on them, pushed out of their places by the naughty sprite. These were his works by day. During the night he was still more active; and frequently, when the workmen came to renew their labours in the morning, they would find the greater part of the work done on the previous day all destroyed and cast down to the ground.

At last, so palpable was it that some unseen hand was at work frustrating their efforts, and that the accidents and mischief were caused by some supernatural power, that the head man of the work, getting quite disheartened at seeing day after day his own and his fellow workmen's labours so frustrated, bethought him to apply to the leaden image of Saint Trinion, which Brodar Merune had set up in a shrine close by, and ask the holy man what he had better do. It was the identical image of the saint that Brodar so luckily had in his pocket on the night of the storm.

The saint soon heard the petitions addressed to him, and immediately making his appearance, informed the suppliant foreman that it was the work of the buggane, and gave him the following instructions how to act in order to prevent any further mischief.

In the first place, the building and works must never be left at night; but so soon as the workmen had finished their day's work, some one must mount guard to watch and keep up a blazing fire of wood from the rowan tree, the fumes of which, when burning, would render powerless all fairies, bugganes, or evil spirits of every description. In the daytime every man was to wear in his hat or cap a sprig of the rowan tree, a bunch of wormwood, and a feather from a sea gull's wing, tied together with a strip of the skin taken from the belly of a conger eel. The same charm was to be fixed in the headgear of each of the horses.

This advice of the saint was followed, and both plans adopted with perfect success, the buggane's power being completely checkmated thereby as promised by the holy man. The building of the church from this time forth made great and rapid progress.

The buggane, possessed of an energy and perseverance worthy of a better cause, never for one instant ceased watching; but while the men and the horses were protected by the charm in their hats and headgear they were safe against his designs.

Sometimes a man grew careless and laid aside his hat and its protecting sprigs, and so surely as any one did so some fatality would happen to him. After some time the men, learning by experience the consequences of neglect, took care to keep their charms always in their hats, and their hats always on their heads. At night the smoke and fumes of the burning rowan-tree wood drove him far from the building, for he could not approach or come in contact with its mystic odours.

Night after night did the persevering little buggane hover round and round the now rapidly progressing church, keeping a sharp eye upon his enemy the watchman. At last, after a long while, and just as the church was on the point of completion, his vigilance and pertinacity were rewarded. One night an opportunity presented itself, which he lost not one moment in taking advantage of. Great efforts had been made by all hands to get the building completed by a certain time, as Brodar Merune had sent word that he intended to come specially to the Isle of Man to be present at the opening and consecration of the church when finished; and the day being fixed, the work was hurried on at the last so as to have all ready by the day of his expected arrival. Every one had been very hard at work all one day to get the roof covered in, and at nightfall it was very nearly completed; only some very trifling matters being left undone, which the foreman himself intended to come early the next morning, and finish before the arrival of the abbot and priests from Saint Germains and Rushen Abbey, with Brodar Merune and many other nobles, for the consecration ceremonies.

The watchman on duty that night had been one of those engaged hard at work all day, for every man that could be got had been employed in the finishing of the church, and the preparations for the morrow's services. The poor fellow was quite tired out with his labours, so after making up a roaring fire of the rowan-tree wood, he thought he might safely take a short nap—just a few winks and a nod—to recruit exhausted nature. He lay down near the fire, and made himself as comfortable as circumstances would permit. He was soon sound asleep and snoring. Now at last the buggane's opportunity had arrived, and all his patience was about to receive its reward in success.

The watchful little sprite had been closely eyeing his enemy, regarding every movement of the man. No sooner did he lie down and fall asleep than the buggane hastened to summon a number of his brother elves, and proceeded, with their help, to work out his own long-cherished revenge.

As long as the fire burned they could do nothing, so their first efforts were directed to extinguish it. One little buggane, more knowing than the others, raised a great wind, which blew the flames and made the fire burn briskly, and the dreaded rowan-tree wood was quickly consumed, all the elfin throng taking care to keep at a respectful distance. and on the windward side of the fire, so as not to get within reach of its magic vapours. The watchman was tired, and slept soundly in spite of the wind and the crackling and roaring of the fierce burning fire, and not waking up to add more fuel, it soon burnt itself out. As the fire got lower and lower, the bugganes drew nearer and nearer, and became more daring. At last all was out except a few dying embers. The elves warily approached quite close, and, following the example of the knowing little fellow who raised the wind, they all began spitting on the ashes till every spark was quenched.

The moment the last spark died out they gave a loud unearthly yell, which awoke the sleeping watchman, who was frightened out of his wits at seeing himself surrounded by such a number of horrid-looking little bugganes, dancing, leaping, shouting, and turning somersaults, that would have made a modern acrobat or music-hall gymnast give up his profession in despair of ever being able to equal.   He looked all round for a way to escape, but before the poor fellow could gain the door and rush out of the building, they all together lifted the roof off the church and dashed it to the ground in ten thousand pieces, burying the unlucky watchman in the ruins.

The zealous foreman of the works was the first to arrive at the church in the early morning, and when he drew near he soon discovered what the bugganes had done, and that Saint Trinion's foe had been as good as his word.

Not seeing anything of the watchman, he shouted his name, and was answered by a groan from beneath the ruin of the shattered roof.   He immediately ran off to hasten the arrival of the workmen, with whose assistance he proceeded to extricate their unfortunate comrade from his very unpleasant predicament.   The poor man, though sadly bruised and battered, besides having what few wits he ever possessed frightened out of him, was not killed, and, fortunately, not seriously hurt, having been protected by two large beams, which in falling had done so crosswise (it was supposed by the intervention of Saint Trinion), and formed a shield that prevented the other timbers and materials from crushing or suffocating him.   After some delay and much exertion he was extricated, and having partaken of a refreshing and invigorating cordial, he told them all that had happened, and how the whole church had been filled with " wee folk," who had lifted the roof and destroyed it.

Intelligence of the disaster was immediately despatched to Peel, where Brodar Merune with the monks and abbot of St. Germain's cathedral were preparing to set out in solemn procession to the new church to perform the ceremonies of opening and consecration.

On hearing the news the hot-headed Irish baron swore terribly, and greatly shocked the holy monks and abbot with his *very* strong language. Calling for a horse, he mounted, set off at full gallop, and soon arrived on the spot, where he saw for himself the devastation that had been committed by his old tormentor the buggane and his helpmates.

After going round the building and hearing from the bruised watchman and others the full particulars, he turned to the abbot, who with some of the less corpulent friars, had by that time arrived at the ruined church, and said, addressing his reverence—

" Well, and shure it isn't me that's to blame at all. I've kept my word, your riverence, honour bright. Neither the holy Saint Trinion, nor your own Saint Germain, nor Ould Nick himself, can say I haven't fulfilled me vow. Sorry it is that I am, that so fine and illigant a new chur-uch should be so spoiled intirely ; but there it is, and so it must remain for me, as I've no more purty jewels to sell nor money to spind for new roofs."

" Ah ! but, my son," solemnly rejoined the abbot, who had promised the living of St. Trinion's church to a special friend of his, and had no desire to lose his little bit of patronage, " I cannot consecrate a church with no roof on it, and the blessed Saint Trinion of holy memory expects you to complete him a proper church and shrine in accordance with your vow."

" Faith, so I did," replied Brodar; "and if that holy and sainted individual cannot look after his own interests sharp enough to prevent a dirty lot of little spalpeen Manx bugganes from playing such divarshions with it when it is done, it's no fault of mine, and bad cess to the groat more that I'll spind on it at all. If he wants a roof to cover his shrine he had better put one on himself, for I shan't."

So saying he remounted his horse and rode towards Peel, leaving the abbot and the monks all contemplating the ruined building.

" Och ! but if iver they make a saint of me," he muttered as he rode along—" and it's small chance of that same, I'm thinking—but if iver they do, I'll take better care of the church that may be built for me than to let a blackguard little buggane play such bedivilment with it as that, indade."

Brodar Merune was quite inexorable on the subject of restoring the roof of the church, therefore the abbot, desirous both of pleasing Saint Trinion and saving his *protégé* from disappointment on the matter of his expectant living, applied to Jarl Haco, asking him to do the necessary work, promising him a large amount of indulgences and dispensations; but the lord of Grebah loved his money too well, and turned a deaf ear to the venerable man's request.

The building was consequently left in its unfinished state, and so remained for some centuries, going gradually to ruin and decay.

ONG after all about Brodar Merune and the tricks of the buggane had been forgotten and faded from the memory of the Manx people, some worthy and well-disposed persons determined to put the church into a proper state of repair, and render it fit and complete for the services of the neighbourhood, which was getting more populated than when the building was begun, and much in want of church accommodation. Accordingly, after a number of parish meetings, at which steps were taken to raise the needful funds, the good work was commenced; but before much progress had been made, an old crone who lived in a hovel by the roadside, came to Robert Quayle, the DOONEY-MOOAR, or the chief man of the parish, who had been deputed to superintend the work of restoration, and reminded him of the old, forgotten tale of the buggane and his destroying the first roof of the church.

Old Maggie Gill, for such was the crone's name, warned Robert Quayle and all those engaged in the good work that their efforts would be utterly useless, and their labour only thrown away.

The resuscitation of the old tale of the buggane caused much gossip and discussion in all the district round about, and the subject of the completion of the church was on every one's mind.

One day a very sanctimonious old tailor, named Timothy Mylrea, well known in that part of the country, and who was aspiring, if the church was completed, to fill the united offices of clerk and sexton, came to the Dooney-Mooar and told him he had on the previous night dreamed that Saint Trinion himself appeared to him, and said that if he, Timothy Mylrea, would, when the roof was finished, sit in the middle of the aisle during the night and make a pair of red cloth breeches, all complete, and walk nine times round the church, it would for ever frustrate the power of the malignant buggane to destroy the roof or otherwise injure the building, and dispel the charm that had hitherto for so many years either hindered or prevented its completion. He volunteered to do this, provided the coveted appointments of clerk and sexton were bestowed upon him. This was agreed to in the event of his being successful, and the work was commenced and pushed forward to completion. On the evening of the day on which the church roof was finished the valiant Timothy betook himself and his work to Saint Trinion's, and, with the good wishes of all his friends and neighbours, proceeded to make the red cloth breeches.

On entering the church and looking round, he saw that all was right and no one there but himself. He closed the door, lit and fixed three candles, arranged his work around him, sat down cross-legged on the floor, and commenced. Having cut out the breeches, he looked up and down and all about. No one appeared, and he took courage. He began to whistle, but his shrill piping sounded somewhat discordant and strange beneath the groined and arched roof of the church, and it suddenly struck Tim Mylrea that whistling was rather out of place in such an edifice. He threaded his needle and basted his work together. He gave another look around the church, and finding no one appeared, his courage waxed stronger, and he began to sing—

King Orry of old
Was a Viking bold,
And far, far from the North came he ;
His ships full of men—
Ten hundred and ten—
Came sailing straight over the sea.
The sea, the sea,
Came sailing over the sea.

A fierce lot they were
That came with him there,
And sailed up the fair River Lhane ;
All trembled with fear,
And hid, far and near,
From terrible Orry the Dane.
The Dane, the Dane,
From terrible Orry the Dane.

" From whence do you come,
Bold Rover ? " asked one,
" And where is your home—let us know ? "
" My home is now here,
It once was up there,
In the land of cold, frost, and snow."
And snow, and snow,
In the land of cold, frost, and snow.

He stretched forth his sword
As he spoke the word,
And pointed right up in the sky—

> "The fair Milky Way
> Was home yesterday,
> Now here is my home till I die.
> I die, I die,
> Now here is my home till I die."

> Orry ruled in Man,
> And the land began
> To thrive and to flourish with ease ;
> For good laws he made,
> And taught the folks trade,
> And founded the old House of Keys.[1]
> Of Keys, of Keys,
> And founded the old House of Keys.

By the time his song was ended the breeches had far progressed towards completion, for stitching away as fast as his fingers could work, he had got one leg quite finished. Looking round again and seeing no one, neither elf nor mortal, Tim was getting quite elated, and thought it must be all stuff and nonsense about the buggane, and that there were no such things after all. Hearing a noise, he again looked up, and there straight before him, sure enough, was a head, appearing just out of the ground, and grinning most horribly at him with great goggle green eyes, distended nostrils, a wide mouth, and fierce fangish-looking teeth ; altogether about the very ugliest sight Timothy Mylrea had ever beheld.

One glance was sufficient to convince him it was the veritable buggane himself, and that all his ideas of there being no such things were erroneous. But he was a plucky fellow was Tim Mylrea, and continued on with his work, keeping his eyes steadfastly fixed on the breeches and stitching away like a patent sewing machine.

---

[1] The House of Keys is the name of the Manx Parliament, which was originally founded by King Orry the Dane.

TIM MYLREA AND THE BUGANE.

" Timothy Mylrea," shouted the buggane, "what are you doing here?"
Tim took no notice, but went on with his work faster than ever.

" Do you see my head?" said the elf.

" Hee! hee!" replied Tim.

" Do you see my great eyes and my long teeth?" howled the buggane,
getting enraged that the tailor was not frightened.

" Hee! Hee!" again replied the busy man, stopping his work one
instant to snuff his candle with his fingers and pitch the severed wick at the
head before him; after which he went on with the breeches, which were now
nearly completed.

Having by this time risen entirely out of the ground, the ugly little fellow,
now furious at this last mark of Mylrea's contempt, began capering about
in front of him, and grinning in his face all the time in the most hideous
manner.

"Tim, you brute!" yelled the buggane. "You wretch! Do you see
my strong arms, my ten fingers, my sharp nails, my big——"

Ere he could utter another word, up jumped the tailor, and, seizing his
work, rushed as fast as he could out of the church. Hardly had he got
clear of the door than down came the roof with an awful crash, that made
him jump more nimbly than ever he did before. Hearing the fiendish
laugh of the buggane, he bounded off as hard as his legs would carry him,
with the red breeches under his arm, along the road towards Douglas, and
the infuriated little buggane after him. It was run tailor, run buggane.
Away they went. Sure mortal man never ran so quick as poor, terrified
Timothy, who, had he been possessed of the "three legs of Man," could
not have got over the ground faster than he did with two.

Turning his head once to look over his shoulder, he saw his horrid,
raving pursuer close upon his heels, with extended jaws and panting forth
dreadful suffocating, sulphurous fumes that would have choked poor Mylrea
had he not kept out of their reach. The buggane's hands were stretched
forth, his claw-armed fingers were ready to clutch and tear him to pieces.
The poor fellow's breath was almost gone, and he thought he really must

give up and fall into the terrible little creature's power, when at a turn of the road he caught sight of the Kirk Braddon before him, and, taking fresh courage and putting on a spurt, he redoubled his efforts.

If only he could reach the church he would be safe he knew, so he took fresh heart and made one more last effort. Running with increased speed the last few yards, he reached the churchyard wall, and, springing over like a deer into the consecrated enclosure, sank exhausted on the ground.

There, beneath the shadow of the church and once on holy soil, he felt safe from all the bugganes and elfins in the island. After taking a few breaths he looked up, and there on the wall could he see his arch enemy grinning, if possible, more horribly than ever, and spitting at him with all his might a perfect shower of sparks and liquid fire.

Fearing the little brute might injure him if any of his hellish spittle reached him, he got up and staggered nearer the church, where he lay down, crouching close to the sacred edifice, and just beneath the chancel window. The buggane, seeing his intended victim had really escaped, gave full vent to his maddened and infuriated rage, which now knew no bounds. After dancing and jumping about on the top of the churchyard wall—he dared not come actually within the precincts of the consecrated ground—and dancing about in the road outside, yelling out most dreadful curses and denunciations to the trembling and exhausted tailor, he made one last expiring effort to annihilate the poor frightened Timothy Mylrea. Seizing his own head in both his hands, and wrenching it off his body, the buggane hurled it over the wall, and, falling at the feet of Mylrea, it exploded like a torpedo, with a report that resounded over the country for miles, echoing from mountain to mountain like a peal of thunder. The noise of the explosion brought the alarmed people from their houses, running from all directions towards whence the noise proceeded to see what calamity had happened. There, in Kirk Braddon churchyard, was Timothy Mylrea found by his neighbours, and, wonderful to say, perfectly unscathed, but most wofully frightened.

On somewhat recovering himself he related all his adventures of the night

9

to the anxious crowd, all eager to hear what had befallen him ; and, sanctimonious and well-conducted man that he was, he actually swore that nothing
on earth should ever tempt him to volunteer to face the fairies or bugganes
again, and that as long as he lived he would give the roofless church of
Saint Trinion as wide a berth as possible.

THE BUGGANE'S LAST SHOT.

A long discussion ensued among the heads of the parish as to what had
caused him to fail at the last moment, as he had evidently up to the time
of leaving the church complied with the instructions Saint Trinion had given

when he appeared to him in his dream and told him to make the red breeches. While the argument was going on the parson took up the nether garments to examine them, when he discovered that they were all complete, *except one solitary button*, which Mylrea had omitted to sew on, in his hurry to leave the church and get away from the little grinning buggane.

Whether, if he had not forgotten the button, the fully completing the red breeches would have broken the charm of the buggane's power and driven him from the church for ever, was long an open question, and one frequently discussed over many a glass of grog. Certain it is, however, that no one else has ever since attempted either to replace the roof on Saint Trinion's church or to exorcise the buggane that even to this day is said to haunt the ruins.

     ✤   ✤   ✤   ✤   ✤   ✤

The roofless church, now a mere picturesque ruin, stands in a field a little way from the roadside on the highway between Douglas and Peel, as a lasting memorial of

𝔗𝔥𝔢 𝔟𝔲𝔤𝔤𝔞𝔫𝔢'𝔰 𝔳𝔬𝔴, 𝔱𝔥𝔞𝔱 𝔖𝔞𝔦𝔫𝔱 𝔗𝔯𝔦𝔫𝔦𝔬𝔫 𝔰𝔥𝔬𝔲𝔩𝔡
𝔫𝔢𝔳𝔢𝔯 𝔥𝔞𝔳𝔢 𝔞 𝔴𝔥𝔬𝔩𝔢 𝔠𝔥𝔲𝔯𝔠𝔥 𝔦𝔫
𝔈𝔩𝔩𝔞𝔫 𝔙𝔞𝔫𝔫𝔦𝔫.

Also published by Llanerch:

THE FOLK-LORE OF THE ISLE OF MAN
A. W. Moore.

SYMBOLISM OF THE CELTIC CROSS
Derek Bryce.

THE TOMBS OF THE KINGS:
AN IONA BOOK OF THE DEAD
John Marsden.

BRITISH GOBLINS: THE REALM OF FAERIE
Wirt Sykes.

THE LIFE OF ST. COLUMBA
Adamnan.

CELTIC FOLK TALES from Armorica
F. M. Luzel.

THE CELTIC LEGEND OF THE BEYOND
Anatole LeBraz.

For a complete list of small-press editions and facsimile reprints, history, legend, mysticism, write to LLANERCH PUBLISHERS, Felinfach, Lampeter, DYFED. SA48 8PJ.